1000 DETAILS
IN LANDSCAPE
ARCHITECTURE

1000 DETAILS

A SELECTION OF THE WORLD'S MOST INTERESTING LANDSCAPING ELEMENTS

IN LANDSCAPE

FRANCESC ZAMORA MOLA, EDITOR

ARCHITECTURE

FIREFLY BOOKS

A FIREFLY BOOK

Published by Firefly Books Ltd. 2012

First printing

Publisher Cataloging-in-Publication Data (U.S.)

Mola, Francesc Zamora.
1000 details in landscape architecture : a selection of the world's most interesting landscaping elements / Francesc Zamora Mola, editor.
[292] p. : ill. (chiefly col.) ; cm.
Summary: A reference catalog to the aesthetic and technical features of outstanding landscape designs chosen from around the world; examines landscape architecture as an artistic application that evolves as plants grow, environmental conditions change, and people use the space.
ISBN-13: 978-1-77085-040-8
1. Architectural design. I. One thousand details in landscape architecture. II. Title.
712 dc23   SB472.M653 2012

Library and Archives Canada Cataloguing in Publication

1000 details in landscape architecture : a selection of the world's most interesting landscaping elements / Francesc Zamora Mola, editor.
ISBN 978-1-77085-040-8
1. Landscape architecture. I. Mola, Francesc Zamora
II. Title: One thousand details in landscape architecture.
SB472.3.0635 2012   712   C2012-903708-7

Published in the United States by
Firefly Books (U.S.) Inc.
P.O. Box 1338, Ellicott Station
Buffalo, New York 14205

Published in Canada by
Firefly Books Ltd.
66 Leek Crescent
Richmond Hill, Ontario L4B 1H1

Cover design: Erin R. Holmes

Printed in China

This book was developed by:
LOFT Publications, S.L.
Via Laietana 32, 4º, of. 92
08003 Barcelona, España
Tel.: +34 93 268 80 88

Editorial Coordinator: Aitana Lleonart Triquell
Editors: Cristina Paredes Benítez, Francesc Zamora Mola
Art Direction: Mireia Casanovas Soley
Design and Model-making coordination: Claudia Martínez Alonso
Model-making: Yolanda G. Román
Model-making assistant: Alba Rojas Sánchez
Translation: Cillero & de Motta

INTRODUCTION   6

STRUCTURES
    Retaining Walls and Screens
        Retaining Walls   8
        Screens   22
    Surface and Paving
        Materials   26
        Design Elements   58
    Fences, Guardrails and Railings
        Fences   68
        Guardrails   76
        Railings   82
    Decks, Platforms and Boardwalks   84
        Decks and Flooring   84
        Seafront and Riverside Boardwalks   92
    Pedestrian Bridges and Lookouts   98
    Urban Furniture and Public Art
        Urban Furniture   114
        Public Art   136

IRRIGATION DESIGN
    Irrigation and Storm Water Management   148
    Reclamation of Disturbed Landscapes   154

LIGHTING DESIGN
    Lighting Fixtures   158
    Lighting Effects   170

PLANTING
    Selection and Use of Trees, Plants, Shrubs and Herbs   182
    Planting Design Types   200

POOL DESIGN AND WATER FEATURES
    Pools   234
    Water Features   260

PHOTO CREDITS   284

INTRODUCTION

Landscape architecture applies cultural, artistic, technical, and scientific knowledge to the design of an open space, often integrated into the urban fabric. In this case, the goal is usually to bring the city closer to nature. Through a commitment to preserve or improve the environment for human use and enjoyment, landscape architects take on the responsibility to create environments that, beyond their aesthetics and functions, show an appreciation and understanding of natural processes. These professionals thrive to bring together land and man-made objects, usually with striking, creative imagination. The object of their work can be as varied as parks, gardens, waterfronts, courtyards, open spaces around public institutions, schools, hotels, hospitals, and airports. With the densification of cities and the lack of vacant spaces, landscape architects can see their territory of expertise expand to areas above ground level, such as vertical gardens and rooftops.

Regardless of the project type, the analysis of the site and the mapping of its features are the beginning of a creative process that finishes with thorough detailing that, in turn, makes a landscape unique. This book is a compendium of examples that show how details help reinforce the general design concept and achieve a specific desired effect. It takes you on a journey across the aesthetic, functional and construction aspects of landscape architecture to demonstrate how powerful design features can transform thematic ideas into awe-inspiring realities. Based on the existing conditions of a specific site, landscape architects use their creative abilities and knowledge to construct their ideas through a design development that culminates with the selection of materials and the design of construction details. These details, which are key to the success of the project, can reinforce design ideas by means of the continuity and discontinuity of patterns, contribute to the overall form and geometry of the design, be designed to be long-lasting and flexible while enhancing the general design, and anticipate the maintenance requirements to minimize future disruptions and maximize cost effectiveness.

The materials included here have been selected for their capacity to inspire and to propose innovative ideas about how to approach the design or construction of various aspects of landscape projects. The book is divided into the following sections: Structures, which includes retaining walls and screens; surface and paving; fences, guardrails and railings; decks, platforms and boardwalks; pedestrian bridges and lookouts; and urban furniture and public art; Irrigation Design; Lighting Design; Pool Design and Water Features; and Planting. The latter includes comprehensive information on the selection and use of trees, plants, shrubs and herbs and examples of planting design types.

The details, in numerical order, are illustrated with color photographs, site plans, sections and numerous construction details. The images are accompanied by comprehensive captions that are, on some occasions, formulated as tips. This book is invaluable for architecture, garden, and landscape design students as well as for professionals, who will find this book useful not only for understanding the work of the best contemporary landscape architects, but also as an inspirational tool for their own design work.

0001 The architects 1:1 landskab believe that for a space to have a strong identity it should find a simple idea that develops and supports all aspects of the project, as in this garden in Chaumont-sur-Loire, France.

0002 The design of the Vienna Airport Tower Plaza, a construction by 3:0 Landschaftsarchitektur, creates a strong contrast between the retaining walls formed by gabions filled with rubble and the fine texture of the gravel used in the plaza.

0003 For 100 Landschaftsarchitektur, beauty is appreciated in the moment right between the onset and decline. In the Jardin de la Connaissance (garden of knowledge), this transition is shown using books as a building material on which mushrooms are grown and the life cycle is recreated.

0001

0002

0003

Sketch

0004

0004 In the General Maister Memorial Park, Bruto Landscape Architecture studio resolved the margins of the river by designing a multifunctional space that serves as a connection between two parts of the city as well as flood protection.

0005 According to Batlle i Roig Arquitectes, the definition of the boundaries builds the place. A boundary is not always a barrier, but it always highlights a difference, a special feature or an exclusion. Its ability to comparatively use spaces attributively is what makes a boundary effective.

0006 According to the architect Beth Galí, memorials and monuments to the victims of war, such as Fossar de la Pedrera in Barcelona, Spain, are sensitive issues. This old quarry converted into a garden was the argument used to evoke emotion and knowledge of the recent history of a country.

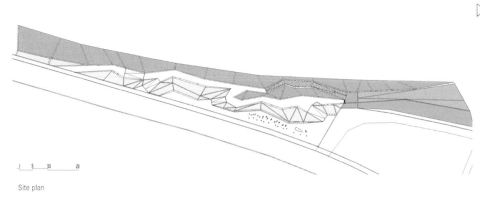

Site plan

0005

0006

0007 Plants are one of the main elements of the landscape and become fixtures of the land. Bruto Landscape Architecture designed an innovative green space to reduce costs and protect the steep slopes on the roof of Hotel Sotelia.

0008 More and more often, the practice of architecture merges with the landscape. In Wellness Orhidelia, designed by Bruto Landscape Architecture, the landscape is contained by inclined planes and is higher up than the installations, giving it an important role.

0009 For Francis Landscapes Sal. Offshore, limitations can play in our favor. In this private residence, the steps formed by rocks of the garden have proved an attractive solution that has avoided the need for retaining walls.

0010 The goal for Francis Landscapes Sal. Offshore when designing the outdoor spaces of this home was to preserve the natural appearance of the landscape with a minimal impact. The retaining walls of the slope integrate the pool into a display of beautiful contrasts.

0011 For Habitat Landscape Architects, the reuse and recycling of materials is important. For the Vredenburg Reserve on the West Coast of South Africa, the rock was reused to fill the gabions forming the retaining walls.

0012 A tight budget may result in a new solution in the use of materials. These large pots by GRC, called Stensjö Planters by the Gora Art & Landscape designers and landscapers, can be used as large containers.

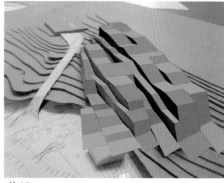

Model

0009

0010

0011

0012

0013

0014

0015

0013 The slope of the East Side Gallery Park has been overcome by the use of ramps between the road along the river and the historical level of the park. The ramps, designed by Häfner/Jiménez Büro für Landschaftsarchitektur, form small retaining walls.

0014 Corten steel sheets contain the vegetation areas of the walkway of the Spandau Citadel, designed by Häfner/Jiménez Büro für Landschaftsarchitektur. These elements help to define the path in relation to the water and land.

0015 To take advantage of the natural morphology of the terrain, Ioakim-Loizas Architects Engineers built a bridge at a higher level and selected the vegetation located on the retaining walls. The structure is concealed and returned to nature.

0016 The retaining walls of this Ioakim-Loizas Architects Engineers project, made with stones, mark the border between the urbanized area and the vegetated area.

0017 Designer Alice Größinger, of Idealice, designed a landscape to bridge the 13-foot (4 m) space of the LKH Klagenfurt Hospital courtyard in Austria. An accessible space and garden for the hospital canteen has been created.

0018 For landscape artist Jos van de Lindeloof, the versatility of the Dutch landscape is an important source of inspiration, such as in these small retaining walls.

0019 KLA Kamphans Landscape Architecture had to take into account existing trees and structures before locating the pool. The problem was solved with some retaining walls that were adapted to the terrain.

0020 The members of the Isthmus Urban Design | Landscape Architecture studio place importance on evaluating how the spaces, vegetation, natural elements and materials interact over time. The breakwater blocks of the Oriental Bay have been integrated into the landscape.

0021 The objective of separating bus traffic from the pedestrian area of the Vincent Lunge Plaza was achieved thanks to black granite walls arranged in a zig-zag design. Landskap Design has managed to facilitate the passage of more than 10,000 pedestrians who pass through this plaza daily.

0022 The design of the Rain Garden in the Oregon Convention Center in Portland, by Mayer/Reed architects, shows how a circuit brimming with plants located between walls and buildings can clean and treat rainwater.

0023 For MADE associati | architettura and paesaggio, building landscapes means working with the land and developing its ability to generate new land. These operations, such as Corten steel retaining walls along the pier, create visual connections and generate new sensory experiences.

0024 The Willamette National Cemetery is a critical intersection where nature meets culture. Intervention in this space, the work of Mayer/Reed, and the design of the walls that define the pathways respect the natural environment and integrate it into people's needs.

0021

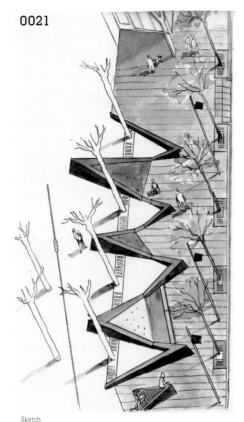

Sketch

0022

▽

Sketch

0023

0024

3-D representation

0025 Working with the landscape can really ingrain the past and create new memories. History has an important role in the design of the Isivivane Freedom Park, South Africa, a project by Newtown Landscape Architects. Natural materials help to link memories to visions of the future.

0026 In the projects by McGregor Coxall, such as Ballast Point Park in Sydney, Australia, new, innovative ways of using building materials are explored, as are even simpler methods, such as a gabion wall.

0027 For Newtown Landscape Architects, the design of S'khumbuto Freedom Park in Pretoria, South Africa, was a beautiful and functional landscape, symbolically powerful and artistically relevant.

0028 The Nieuwe Hollandse Waterlinie, designed by Okra landscape architects, is one of the limits that mark the boundary between wet and dry. In specific places this line is removed, showing the reason for the barrier.

0029 Simplicity is one of the maxims of oslund.and. assoc. Gold Medal Park is one of the best examples of this principle. The use of Corten steel in the containment area of this gentle hill was a wise move, making the final result more attractive.

0030

0031

3-D representation

0032

0030 Here, Okra has successfully integrated protection into a space that can be used and enjoyed by all of the population. The materials used in the quay wall in Doesburg, the Netherlands, connects the historic center with the IJssel River without major aesthetic disruptions.

0031 A garden should never be merely a decorative accessory to a building, but the garden and building should complement each other and express their qualities. The urban garden and infrastructure of Matera, Italy, a work by Osa architettura e paesaggio, manages to highlight the green spaces thanks to its distribution in lots.

0032 To ensure permanence over the life of a project, R&R Rencoret y Ruttimann architects build fixtures that create a new structure on the site. Other variable factors will be developed over time without affecting the initial concept.

0033 It is important to choose materials that respond to local conditions. In this park by Rankinfraser Landscape Architecture, the use of the leftover stone from the excavation and Corten steel in the walls ensures the durability of materials over time.

0034 It is important to work with nature, but avoid trying to be exactly like it. In the Municipal Cemetery of Malla, Spain, RGA architects arranged walls with a twofold function: to secure the natural terrain and define pathways.

0035 Restrictions, whether they are related to budgets, regulations or customer demands, must be turned into challenges. In the LAC+USC Medical Center in Los Angeles, California, designed by Rios Clementi Hale Studios, walls and ramps were used to make the building accessible and a small green area was created.

0036 It is important to consider climate changes and the evolution of the seasons. In this factory next to the water, Schweingruber Zulauf Landschaftsarchitekten created an exterior space that adapts to the changing landscape caused by the rise and fall of the tide.

0037 These concrete walls by Shades of Green mark the levels of the slope. The plants, chosen to avoid saturating the space, visually emphasize the different terraces.

0038 The stones of the walls of the outer areas of this house designed by Simon Rackham, in Epidavros, Greece, are of local origin. The use of locally sought materials and native vegetation assists the sustainability of the ecosystems.

0036

0037

▽

0038

0039

0040

0041

0042

0043

0039 To protect the gap between the road and the entrance to this residence in Punta Ballena, members of Verdier Landscape Design Studio opted for a neat retaining wall and rocks that appear to have been on the site forever. This solution is simple and has a minimalist aesthetic.

0040 The design of the exterior areas of this residential and tourist resort of Bali Alila Villas Uluwatuse was carried out with the aim of integrating the architecture into the landscape. WOHA's concept reproduces the typical limestone terraces in the area.

0041 The exterior area of Walden Studio, designed by Jensen Architects, consists of a retaining wall using stone in two different ways. This solution provides a dynamic space that fuses the architecture with the vineyards that surround the building.

0042 Lucien Rose Residential Complex is adjacent to Thabor Park in Rennes, France, in a lot with several levels. Materials such as stone walls and the color beige unify the style of the complex, designed by Atelier du Pont.

0043 The efficiency of gabion walls, a sort of metal cage with stones inside, has turned this element into one of the most-used exterior spaces. In Ballas Point Park, designed by McGregor Coxall, the gabions define the uneven levels.

0044 Sandra Aguilar has developed the ability to observe and capture opportunities to implement appropriate and ductile solutions. These artificial embankments contain the terrain and fit into the landscape without being too abrupt.

0044

0045 Carve architects do not think it is necessary to create a brand; it will form itself thanks to the experience and the work of each landscape designer. This playground in Melis Stokepark meets complex demands, but it has ended up being used by all park users.

0046 For Alice Größinger, of Idealice, there are several steps between a visionary idea and its realization. This screen, located on the Glacis Beisl restaurant patio in Vienna, Austria, has been conceived as a painting that is growing.

0047 The landscape architect Lodewijk Baljon devised a screen with a million LEDs to provide motion and identity to Apeldoorn Station Square, the Netherlands. The moving images symbolize the landscape and travel.

0048 According to Karres en Brands Landschapsarchitecten, it is important to experience and enjoy beauty without having thought about it in the design process. The texture and shadows that are projected on this screen create an unexpected effect.

▽

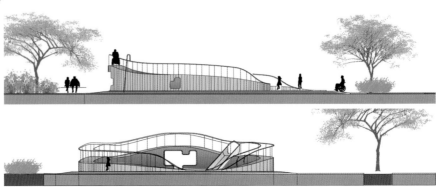

Elevations

▽

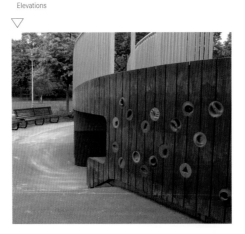

0049

0049 According to architects Mayer/Reed, it is necessary to express the spirit of the most common building materials in an original way. In this way, the artistic expression is present in all forms of a constructed environment.

0050 The stone gabion walls in the Meerterpen cemetery, designed by Jos van de Lindeloof, are elements that have twofold functions: screens that separate spaces and small niches.

0051 According to Thomas Oslund, from oslund.and. assoc., simplicity should always be prioritized over complexity. In the Medtronic Corporation Patent Garden, the simplicity in the design of all elements can be appreciated, from the form to the location of a screen.

0050

0051

0052 R&R Rencoret y Ruttimann architects worry not only about the broad outlines of the project but pay attention to detail in all the elements, such as divisions and screens. The materials and finishes should be consistent with the function.

0053 Taylor Cullity Lethlean architects designed these screens for the Métis International Garden Festival. These festivals are a good incentive for creativity, and the resulting projects explore the relationships between art, design and science.

0054 For RMP Stephan Lenzen Landschaftsarchitekten, landscape architecture is not art, but rather a combination of brilliant and creative engineering and craftsmanship in a horticultural work. The Dyck Field functional screens are evidence of this.

0055 Architectural elements in parks and gardens can have meaning beyond the purpose for which they were designed. The bright red color screens next to the trees and flowerbeds in the Thomas Balsley Associates project give the space personality.

0056 Areas in the outskirts of cities are underused. The Shades of Green studio has created screens that function as extensions of the open-air houses and encourage communication in the neighborhood.

0057 For Shades of Green, it is important to use vertical spaces, especially in small spaces. These surfaces can be important elements of the design of an exterior space. In this case, the decoration is applied to the wall.

0058

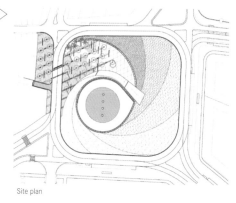

Site plan

0059

0058 A small gabion wall separates the fountain from the pedestrian area of the Plaza dels Països Catalans de Vila-seca, Spain. This element, designed by Arteks, acts as a visual and physical separation, but its low height allows the conceptual unity of the ensemble.

0059 The mesh used in the Spidernetthewood project limits the growth of the vegetation and acts as screens. Over time, the work of R&Sie(n) will form a labyrinth.

0060 Dynamic spaces emerge when two different languages are contrasted, such as structured and organic elements. In Nedre Foss urban park in Oslo, Norway, by 1:1 landskab, the asphalt paving and polyhedral concrete mounds are prominent features.

0061 Construction materials, especially those used in paving, must be of a high quality, local in origin and age beautifully. In the Charlotte Ammundsens Square in Copenhagen, Denmark 1:1 landskab has used masonry in two colors that meet these criteria.

0062 In the paving of the Sophienborg Elementary School in Hillerød, Denmark, traditional materials, such as stone, have been combined with more modern materials. 1:1 landskab architects manage to highlight the identity and beauty of both.

0063 In this Zen space, located in front of a restaurant in the historic center of Kyoto, Japan, a water scene is represented without this element, following the tradition of Zen gardens. A modern twist is provided by the metal 1moku co., which is used in the flowerbeds of the trees.

0064 This garden, designed by 1moku co., combines large slabs of white stone, rough stone and green grass. This contrast of materials and the sinuous lines of the walkway, which symbolize the course of a river, create a pleasant and welcoming space.

0065 100 Landschaftsarchitektur recovered a fresh view to be able to imagine a garden anywhere, including the urban landscapes of our cities. In the Garden of Color temporary project, the concrete floor for the new garden has been marked with tape to delineate the streets.

0063

0064

0065

0066 You do not need to plant a large number of plants to create a harmonious garden. In the courtyard of this Berlin home, 100 Landschaftsarchitektur architects combine the textures of the stones, gravel and vegetation.

0067 The architects of Vito Acconci studio designed a changing landscape, the Courtyard in the Wind, in Munich, Germany. The turbine of an adjacent tower generates electricity that rotates the ring.

0068 Shopping malls use powerful visual strategies to encourage consumption: lights, screens, etc. The urban spaces of the BTC shopping mall in Ljubljana, Slovenia designed by Bruto Landscape Architecture, require a more provocative design with bright colors and contrasting materials.

0069 The floor covering of the Expo Zaragoza 2008 Park in Spain, designed by Batlle i Roig Arquitectes, is defined by large colored circles that are mottled by the round shadows from the roof covering.

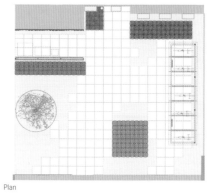

Plan

0070

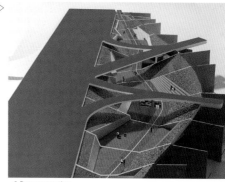

3-D representation

0071

0072

0070 Even more than its appearance, how an exterior space works is very important. In Šentvid Park, Slovenia, a work by Bruto Landscape Architecture, the paving is arranged so that it directs the movement of pedestrians and cyclists and adds dynamism.

0071 The aim of the architect Beth Galí in the HafenCity Hamburg project in Germany was to find the human scale. The paving, which combines slabs and stones, helps to create an easily recognizable space and improves the orientation.

0072 The change in the color of the paving of the Elwood Promenade in Melbourne, Australia, divides the intersection of the bicycle lane with the pedestrian area. For ASPECT Studios, it is a way to communicate and define the uses of the road without being overly dogmatic or compromising aesthetic quality.

0073 This design by Bruto Landscape Architecture for Čufar Square, Slovenia is based on making the area more dynamic. On a shoestring budget, which was almost entirely spent on water spouts, the designers used paint to make the paving more modern.

0073

Collage

0074 The renowned landscape architect Paolo Bürgi conducted a research project, Venustas et Utilitas, which explored the aesthetics of cultivating spaces in an urban environment. This field became a checkerboard, stimulating curiosity among viewers and forcing them to ask questions.

0075 Monseigneur Charbonneau Plaza in Montreal, Canada, a design by Cardinal Hardy, plays with paving stones to divide and separate the plaza from the road. Only stones have been used to mark out the tree pits or boundaries.

0076 With this installation, Cardinal Hardy commemorates the famous John Lennon song written during his 1969 bed-in with Yoko Ono. Slabs on the ground create a paving where you can read the words "Give Peace a Chance," the name of the installation, in several languages.

0077 The visibility of a project is part of its success. To unify an area with 19 office buildings, members of Burger Landschaftsarchitekten used polygonal stone slabs separated by strips of grass.

0078 Materials define spaces. In Dorchester Square, Montreal, the Cardinal Hardy team has used noble stones to cover an area once occupied by a cemetery. The granite of the cartographic symbols of the cemetery honors those who lie beneath the surface.

0079 The floor covering of Columbusplein, by Carve, revitalizes an urban plaza and extends its use to different audiences, including children.

0080 The Piazza Castello is located in front of Congress City in Lugano, Switzerland and covers an underground parking lot. The apparent simplicity of the paving of the square, which has become a meeting place, is interrupted at nightfall with the presence of blue LED lights scattered throughout the space.

0081 The conscious choice of materials provides identity to the project. In the walkway along the fjord of the city of Aalborg, Denmark, tarmac, steel, cement and wood have been used. In addition, C. F. Møller architects added references to the sea, such as the forms of waves on the paving.

0074

Site plan

0075

0076

0077

0078

0079

0080

0081

0082 The silhouette of this man, an Earthscape design, was created from different plants. This project is part of the activities of a foundation that attempts to spread the benefits of coffee to society.

0083 The playground area of the Flora Nativa (native flora) park, designed by Fabio Márquez, has two types of paving: rubber for children's areas and earth. The cement separates and defines this area of this circular-shaped park.

0084 In this rest area off a highway, C. F. Møller shows how combining vegetation and asphalt can result in a dynamic and original space.

0085 The Japanese Architects at Earthscape include children's play areas in their projects, often based on traditional games such as Amidakuji. These areas seem to emerge from the paving, rather than being arranged on the surface.

0086 For Gerhard Rennhofer, the objectives of a project must include room for future needs, and it is not necessary that all areas of an outdoor space serve a purpose. The stone slab paving of the square can be adapted to multiple uses.

0087 To avoid monotony in urban areas, you can play with forms and inclinations. Here, the architects at Earthscape transform what would have been a non-descript concrete square into a dynamic surface that includes a play area.

0088 Changing the layout of urban elements, such as these covers concealing access to water or telephone services, is an opportunity to make the paving more dynamic, such as in this design by East, but it must be incorporated perfectly so that it fits into the space.

0089 On Sutton High Street, in London, England, special pieces of granite have been used with a surface that facilitates water drainage in a sloping surface. This project was a work of East.

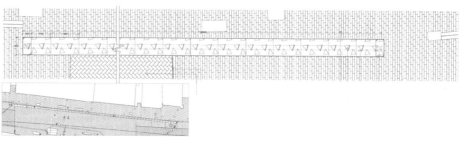

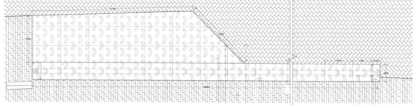

Construction details

0090

0091

0092

0093

0094

0090 Certain garden materials have a greater need for water. In this private garden, designed by Habitat Landscape Architects, gravel and stone have been used to reduce the surface area that requires watering without compromising the space's personality.

0091 Landscape designs can be adapted to the vernacular architecture and to local materials, achieving landscapes better suited to the environment. This manure paving used by Habitat Landscape Architects also repels insects.

0092 For Habitat Landscape Architects, it is important to keep in mind the actual nature and transformations that each project will undergo over time. Using durable materials, such as stones and bricks, increases the strength of the landscape.

0093 The materials used in this part of the garden, a work by Francis Landscapes Sal. Offshore, create a contrast between the purity of the straight lines of the stone slabs and the naturalness of the white stones. The ensemble creates an area for a quiet break.

0094 The Forum Adlershof square is an open space with paved flooring. Häfner/Jiménez architects designed a surface with lines of concrete that extend across the square and leave room for granite paving on one side and greenery on the other.

0095 One of the maxims of the landscape architecture studio Hosper is: if something doesn't exist, design it. This paving was designed especially so that it could be integrated into the vegetation in some areas.

0095

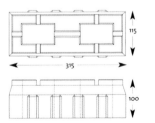

Construction details of the paving pieces

0096 The interior courtyards of the Klagenfurt Hospital in Austria were created from colored stones, creating a friendly and low maintenance space.

0097 The composition of the paving of the HtO Park, in Toronto, Canada, designed by Janet Rosenberg, was inspired partially by the sand dunes. The area around the mounds of grass was paved with large slabs and stones.

0098 Projects must adapt to the environment because, as Janet Rosenberg says, you do not choose the place where you work. For the Town Hall Square in Toronto, situated between a few modern buildings and a historic library, a dispersed weave was chosen for the paving.

0099 A combination of bricks and mortar form an outdoor space in a garden, designed by Jos van de Lindeloof. The difference between the paved area and the garden showcases the most common uses of exterior spaces at home.

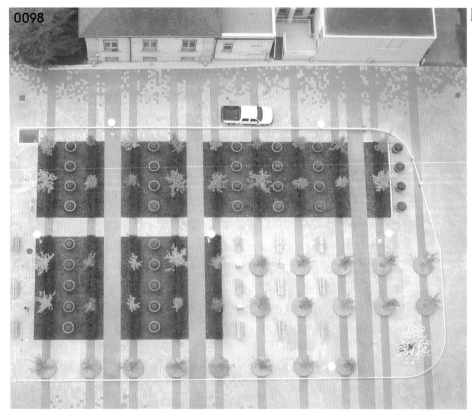

0100

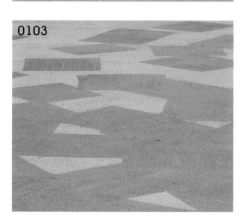

0100 Karres en Brands always suggests reviewing the design, which is one way to learn from one's actions. In this square, stones are combined with asphalt paving, where the name of the street is indicated, to define the pedestrian passage.

0101 This small detail by Jos van de Lindeloof, a few leaves marked on a concrete surface, demonstrates how artistic touches bring practical value to landscape design.

0102 For the inner courtyards of the hospital in Klagenfurt, Austria, a work by Idealice, the studio of architect Alice Größinger, two types of spaces were designed: colored courtyards and, for the hospital areas, more austere areas with more traditional materials.

0103 Cement was used for the paving of this area, which was then swept with brooms to give it its characteristic texture. The idea is the result of improvisation by Karres en Brands architects.

0101

0102

0103

0104

0105

0106

0107

0108

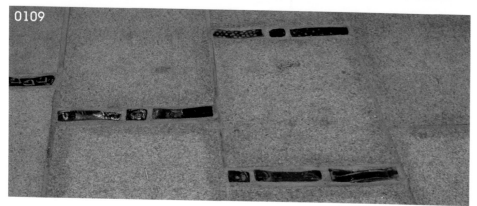

0109

0110

0111

0104 One of the maxims of Landlab is to create space to generate landscape. In Funenpark in Amsterdam, the Netherlands, a dynamic paving in various shades of gray has been designed to provide movement to the circulation areas and create an attractive and less conventional landscape.

0105 The Tracce project, by LAND-I Archicolture, is an installation in which a hand scratching the surface of a garden has been imagined. This project simulates the movement of soil and the discovery of materials under the vegetation, which in this case are fragments of pottery, acorns, bones, etc.

0106 In Colonia di Renesse, the LAND-I Archicolture architects decided to cover the outdoor space with grass and vegetation with the idea of recovering and restoring the links between place, history and community.

0107 In the Oranje Fonds project, in Utrecht, the Netherlands, Landlab architects have used two types of materials for the paving surrounding the landscaped areas: cement for the access, since it is more resistant, and earth for the remaining space, which provides a more natural touch to the complex.

0108 Landlab believes that the soul of a landscape project lies in its details. In the Gooikerspark parking lot in Deventer, the Netherlands, the tarmac covering the surface area has been painted to make it more attractive.

0109 The quality of pavings can be enhanced by additional decorations, such as these ceramic decorations between the joints, the work of Kari Aasen and Eli Veim for The Strand de Landskap Design project. These details improve the visibility of the gray granite.

0110 The painter Kurt Edvin Blix excitedly agreed for one of his works to be the inspiration for the Vejle Traffic Center floor covering, designed by Landskap Design. Six different types of stone from five different countries were used in 45 different ways.

0111 This narrow street in the medieval center of Vejle, Denmark, has a simple but effective design: Landskap Design devised a slope of granite slabs to facilitate the channeling of rainwater to the drain. A 2 3/4-inch (7 cm) wide polished stone strip defines the passage of the water.

0112 A huge vertical gneiss wall was Landskap Design's inspiration for the Årdal Town Hall Square paving. Two types of local stone were used to achieve the parallel appearance.

0113 For Mayer/Reed, it is important to create public spaces for pedestrians, especially with the increasing density of cities. With the renovation of the Eastbank Esplanade in Portland, Oregon, the city now boasts a vibrant and bustling promenade for citizens.

0114 In the exterior area of the Leiden University Medical Center, in the Netherlands, gravel is the protagonist. The quality of the materials can create a significant visual effect that gives personality to the space. In this case, Lodewijk Baljon has used gravel in two colors.

0115 In the Ole Bulls Plass, only two types of stone were used, but Landskap Design decided to show the different surfaces and textures of the stones, rough, uneven, smooth, polished, etc., thus forming a changing landscape that is richer in details.

0116

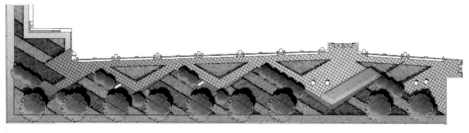

0117

Plan

0118

0119

WATHINTA UMFAZI WATHINTA IMBOKODO
STRIKE THE WOMAN YOU STRIKE THE RO

0116 Although the materials used may be basic and common, a good combination and location can transform a boring space into a suggestive one. Oslund and Associates have achieved a corner that transmits serenity by combining stones of different textures with water and grass.

0117 For Mayer/Reed, it is important to create flexible outdoor spaces where you can collaborate, share, agree on and enjoy the outdoors together. These ideas should be considered when designing a project.

0118 This space, designed by N-tree so that the client could see the moon, stands out for the elegance of the design of the paving. Granite stones were alternated with flat slabs in a checkerboard layout to symbolize a cloud and recreate a celestial space.

0119 In the Moroka Dam Precinct in Soweto, South Africa, Newtown Landscape Architects bring together social and ecological objectives. For the mosaic tiling for the paving, the town got involved to strengthen the sense of belonging to a community and to acquire new skills.

0120 The Afrikaanderplein was an underutilized space in the city of Rotterdam, the Netherlands, when Okra began the renovation. In addition to marking the routes within the park, the tarmac covering also separates the green areas from the central space.

0121 In the remodeling of the historic center of Zutphen, Okra has taken the past into account when choosing the materials. The central part of the streets is made of bricks arranged in the form of a spike. The sides are large granite stones.

0122 The market square in Enschede by Okra Landschapsarchitecten is a flexible space with a changing dynamic. Some elements can be added, removed or changed position. The arrangement of the paving and the combination of stone and tarmac contributes to this dynamic perception.

0123 It's not only children who like to play. The Rehwaldt Landschaftsarchitekten studio used a tarmac pavement and paint as a highlight and to give the place a special identity.

0124 This square, by PEG office of landscape + architecture, uses tiles specifically designed for it. This combination achieves an uneven, lighter result. They are also inclined so that the rain water reaches the plants.

0125 The bus station in Enschede is an urban space that blends with the city. The stations are no longer final destinations, but transit areas and meeting spaces. The floor covering, continuous but with elements that mark the features, adapts to the aesthetics without losing functionality.

0126

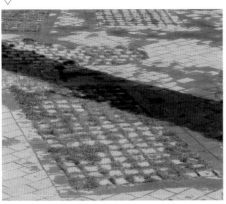

0127

0126 The combination of original and new paving in the monument complex of the churches of San Pere de Terrassa, by RGA Arquitectes, is what adds value and identity to the project.

0127 The Not Garden Project, by PEG office of landscape + architecture, uses common materials to create different spaces. This distribution of areas with gravel and vegetation zones manages, with very little time and investment, to resemble a tended and protected garden.

0128 With suitable paving, a public space takes on a bright atmosphere even without pedestrians. The different blocks of this square, designed by Rijnboutt, are combined with natural stone arranged in lines, creating a beautiful space that is close to people.

0129 Only two colors were used for the materials in the remodeling that the Rijnboutt studio carried out of this square: black and yellow. The choice of colors has revitalized an urban center built in the 70s.

0130 The use of a concrete pavement or its placement can add consistency or generate dynamism and randomness. In Ligapark in Roosendaal, the Netherlands, Rijnboutt architects designed a ground covering that would remain in the background, thus making the other elements of the space stand out.

0131 A classic space need not be boring according to Rijnboutt. The traditional oval composition and resilient and lasting brick pavement in Konigsplein in Ridderkerk, the Netherlands, will form a dynamic space that is ready to become an urban theater.

0132 In the Pliegues Topográficos (topographic folds) project, designer Sandra Aguilar shows how she has designed a second nature: reconciling movement, direction and textures arising from the geomorphology of the territory. These spaces, formed with stones, become observation platforms.

0133 When history is mixed with landscape design, it leaves a permanent mark. In the Hollywood and Vine subway exit in Los Angeles, California, designed by Rios Clementi Hale Studios, the choice of materials is based on the glamour and nostalgia of the movie industry.

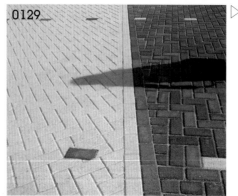

0131

0132

0133

0134

0135

0136

0137

0134 Beyond the ecological reasons for selecting a material, the design should not dictate the choice, whether it is stone, tarmac or concrete, as in the Schmerikon dock. The use of a particular material gives the end result an identity, according to Schweingruber Zulauf Landschaftsarchitekten.

0135 The use of key building materials, such as stone, cement and wood in the outdoor spaces at Fordham University, a work carried out by Sasaki, can create landscapes that are integrated into the environment and provide placid spaces to be enjoyed throughout the year.

0136 Stephen Diamond Associates uses local and re-cycled materials in these courtyards. In this case, recy-cled glass and Irish blue limestone have been chosen. The combination fills these forgotten spaces with life.

0137 The two-colored paving opposite the Royal Dublin Society, by Stephen Diamond Associates, is an abstract interpretation of the relationships and connections of this organization with art, culture, agriculture and the historical use of this site.

0138 To form a path on a farm in Epidavros, Greece, landscape architect Simon Rackham used stone slabs from a nearby quarry. Like many other architects, he says that local resources, materials and plants should be the first choice.

0139 For Shades of Green, it is important that the sur-faces of urban areas are permeable whenever possible to prevent water shortages. This combination of gravel and cement, for example, accomplishes this goal and is elegant, economical and practical.

0140 By placing colored rubber surfaces in this space designed by Stephen Diamond Associates, the impor-tance of aesthetics in the makeup of outdoor spaces is recognized.

0141 The outdoor areas of the IADT campus, designed by Stephen Diamond Associates, were developed as an abstract composition. The combination of materials such as soil or rock connects gardens with walkways.

0142 The installation of green roofs is a challenge that requires the collaboration of the entire design team, in this case the SWA Group. Part of the roof of the California Academy of Sciences is accessible and is therefore paved.

0143 Birk Nielsen, of Sweco Architects, proposed a pleasant space with gardens bounded by curbs and steps that create geometric shapes. From the apartments surrounding the campus, you have a privileged view.

0144 The combination of materials in the paving of the garden area of the Poly International Plaza, designed by SWA Group, transfers visitors to a natural and timeless environment, despite being in a modern office and development center in China.

0145 The art of designing gardens is, according to Birk Nielsen of Sweco Architects, a way to create adventure and to add beauty to spaces for the enjoyment of all.

0146 Cast iron is a durable and resistant material, suitable for the outdoors. In this case, Birk Nielsen of Sweco Architects used this material for paving in the center of Aalborg, Denmark.

0147 The philosophy of Taylor Cullity Lethlean encourages a type of landscape design that brings visitors on a sensory and visual journey, creating spaces that make an instant impression as the landscape grows and matures. The red color of the paving of the Australian Garden is a test of this ideology.

0148 In Sportpark Maselake, in Berlin Spandau, Germany, Topotek designers created a space for practicing athletics, in which the tarmac floor and yellow lines stand out. The architects, however, offer a free use of space.

0149 In the Courtyard Unter den Linden project, Topotek designed an elegant courtyard with light colored organic elements on the dark paving. The drawing can be seen in its entirety from the upper levels of surrounding buildings.

0150 Humor forms part of Topotek's projects. The red color of the ground is the protagonist of this space, the Kaiak Market Parking, where the designers warn users about the possibility of losing their car, if it is also red.

0151 The shortage of available space required precise geometry to be able to plant fruit trees. This provision by Verdier Landscape Design Studio optimizes the number of specimens planted. By placing gravel around the trees, the garden takes on a more poetic dimension.

0152

0153

0154

0155

0152 Gravel paving is suitable for walkways in large parks, as they recreate the forest trails and wild landscapes better than any other materials. PLANT Architect Inc. has used this resource in the Dublin Grounds of Remembrance.

0153 The continuous concrete paving of Union Point Park, designed by GDU, clearly marks the passageways, and because it is smooth, it makes the use of bicycles and skates easier.

0154 In the Largo da Devesa Square, designed by Mateo Arquitectura, in Castelo Branco, Portugal, the traditional Portuguese cobblestone pavements have been restored to form plant and geometric designs.

0155 As part of the remodeling of Gran Vía, one of the most important and longest avenues in Barcelona, Spain, Arriola & Fiol Arquitectes designed the walkways and street furniture. The paving also stands out for the mixture of materials that separate uses: colored tarmac and bricks.

0156 In this Form/Loft 302 project, the 50th anniversary of the discovery of DNA is being celebrated. McGregor Coxall pays tribute to the genetic processes with a floating design and materials such as cement and sandstone.

0157 Bricks and stone are the materials used by Urbanus for Diwang Park B. Their combination creates lanes that cross the park from one end to the other and define the route to follow.

0158 The new tarmac paving of this space, designed by landscape architect Kristine Jensens, can be used as a giant blackboard and acts as a giant canvas on which different forms are drawn with thermoplastic and street paint.

0159 The restoration of the sidewalk of the Mittelstraße has transformed this space for pedestrians with a simple and modern design. The two colors of stones form a striped pavement pattern.

0160 Andrea Cochran has designed outdoor spaces for the Walden Studio that combine earth and gravel with Corten steel sheets. The latter defines the path and frames the landscape of vineyards that surround the complex.

0161 Concrete, brick and earth for the wooded area are the materials used for the paving of the functionally designed Heinz Raspe Square. Narrow metal columns are the elements that distinguish it from other open spaces.

0162 The design of this space in the K-8 campus of Nueva School includes native plants and a channel for collecting rainwater. The elegant design by Andrea Cochran combines large pale-colored slabs with wood and rounded stones that provide the aesthetic counterpoint.

0163 The city center of Aalborg, Denmark, is one of the most important spaces in the city. In this space, several pedestrian streets come together, so there is emphasis on creating a place with its own identity. The quality of materials, such as granite, contributes to the success of the outcome.

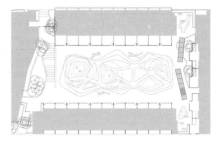

Plan

0159

0160

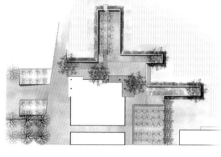

Site plan

0161

0162

0163

Site plan

0164 The rectangular lot that Jacaranda Square occupies, designed by ASPECT Studios, loses rigidity throught the curves incorporated into its design. The brick paving surrounds the lawn area and creates a gentle movement in the accessible area.

0165 Tillner & Willinger designed the new market square in Opfikon, Switzerland. The central red paving is a prominent feature, separating the pergola and wooden floor on one side from the space reserved for the market and other events.

0166 Lundberg Design has designed a garden with different dimensions for this home in Pacific Heights. The aerial view shows gravel, black granite blocks and steel lines. But when passing through the garden, the plan gains volume and becomes a quiet space that is perfect for wandering aimlessly.

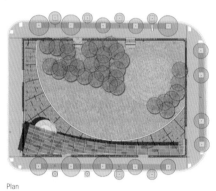

Plan

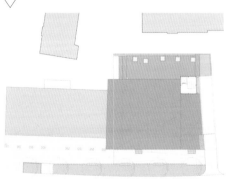

Plan

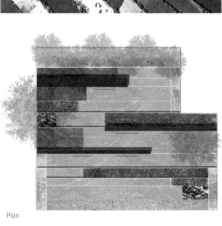

Plan

0167

0167 Scoon residence, by Kendle Design Collaborative, has many elements that contribute to sustainable architecture. In the garden, native plants were chosen and paved areas were kept to a minimum.

0168 The different textures of compacted soil are characteristic of the architecture of the School of Visual Arts, from the Mauricio Rocha Taller de Arquitectura. In the paving, the same materials stand out, as well as stone, which revitalizes and demarcates the paths to the buildings.

0169 HtO is an urban beach that runs along the waterfront in Toronto, Canada. It is a space that adapts to the seasons of the year and offers an urban space for citizens. The combination of materials by Janet Rosenberg + Associates, sand, grass and concrete, adapt to this goal.

0168

0169

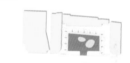

Site plan

0170 Prefabricated blocks have been used for the main entrance of Scoon residence. With these materials, which are resistant and suitable for extreme weather, Kendle Design Collaborative architects reduce the maintenance needs of this area.

0171 The ceramic material of the paving of the new promenade in Benidorm, Spain, is the most attractive element of this new coastline. This promenade establishes a new limit, integrates the different forms of circulation and gives priority to pedestrians.

0170

0171

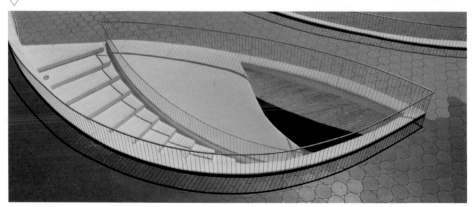

0172 Cardinal Hardy architects dare to play with materials to create dynamic spaces. Mount Royal Park in Montreal, Canada, features grass, slats of wood, surfaces covered with bark, concrete, etc. The combination enhances the final result.

0173 In the courtyard of the LKF clinic in Klagenfurt, Austria, Idealice architects have achieved a good mix of materials that enrich the space visually and also includes vegetation.

0174 Richard Koek designs outdoor spaces using materials honestly, that is, using each of them in the right place. The wooden slat terraces of the De Stadhouder project in Apeldoorn, the Netherlands, are surrounded by a stone border that limits and protects the zones.

0175 The dividers, curbs, pavers and stone blocks dictate the layout of the Lofts Lowney Square. The sculpture of a cherry completes this space designed by Cardinal Hardy.

0176 The slopes and obstacles of the area for skaters of Beatrixpark in Almere, Netherlands, respond to Bureau B+B's desire to reserve spaces for different groups so that everyone can make urban spaces their own.

0177 To give more strength to the context, Burger Landschaftsarchitekten architects propose to clarify and define the connections and relationships with the space. This square uses several elements, such as the slab walls of the decorative fountain, to personalize its image.

0178 Earthscape architects used the vertical part of the steps of this project, located in a former samurai house, such as tables on which to display the chronology and history of the site.

0179 The program of the Las Llamas park includes steps, ramps and stairs. For Batlle i Roig Architects, the uses must rest on the site just as a passing traveler would, that is, originally intended uses can change over time.

0180

0180 In this temporary garden designed by LAND-I Archicolture for the International Garden Festival 2002, held in Quebec, Canada, holes were made in the ground to experiment with shadows. These elements symbolize an archaeological dig.

0181 A space can be multi-functional when several applications and solutions to multiple needs are expected. The curbs of General Maister Memorial Park, a work by Bruto Landscape Architecture, define the path, limit the retaining walls and serve as a support for a bench.

0182 The introduction of a small amphitheater in the square, designed by Ioakim-Loizas Architects Engineers, doubles use of this space: first, a theater area and second, a seating space from which parents can watch their children play.

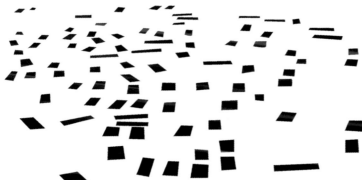

Conceptual diagram

0181

0182

0183

0184

0185

0186

0183 The diversity of elements and textures in this Rankinfraser Landscape Architecture project serves to separate the spaces. The red paving divides the pedestrian area of the park, so the cobblestone curbs did not need to be functional.

0184 The ZOG project, from Rehwaldt Landschaftsarchitekten studio, is distinguished by the elements that outline its walkways. By themselves, the pieces do not define any specific function, but together they give the space a more urban feel.

0185 Metal plates are arranged in an apparently haphazard way at the entrance to the Kalkriese Osnabrück Museum and Park, a work by Schweingruber Zulauf. These elements divide the pathway, and they are simple to install and replace.

0186 The curbs of this landscaped path are barely noticeable. Simon Rackham Landscape Architects Designers decided to give prominence to the form and vegetation and avoided brightly colored materials, opting for a simple white stone.

0187 The outdoor areas of T-Mobile City, a work by RMP Stephan Lenzen Landschaftsarchitekten, the harmony between the pergolas that protect the bicycles and the cement slabs and garden area all stand out.

0188 This urban space, located between the street and the canal, is part of a more complex recovery project of the channels in the city of Mechelen, Belgium. Okra architects have used a different material to highlight the gap between the two ends of the promenade.

0189 The renovation carried out by Landskap Design of the pedestrian access to the cable car station, dating back to 1907, used Art Nouveau decorations as inspiration. The curbs of the sidewalk have rounded shapes and a spiral groove as an ornament.

0190 The significance of certain architectural elements, such as curbs or steps, demonstrate their relative importance. In the Merker Areal Baden, a work by Schweingruber Zulauf architects, the path is delimited despite the snow thanks to the curbs.

0191 The island of Spetses, Greece, is a haven for visitors. Simon Rackham architects chose white stone for the entire perimeter of the pool to highlight the landscape and the light of the Mediterranean Sea. All elements, curbs, steps, benches, etc., are constructed with the same material.

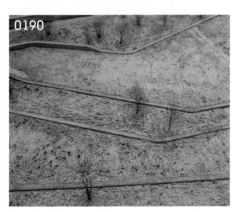

0192 At the entrance of this building, designer Janet Rosenberg has created a friendly space that functions as a waiting and rest area. The concrete cubes and low walls that can be used as seats and benches and the metallic walls of the walkway over the water are prominent features.

0193 In the Topotek Railway Cover project, the slightly sloping orange curbs stand out, which divide the different uses of the space.

0194 The paths of gardens and parks can be outlined in a thousand ways. In this case, Tegnestuen Schul architects ensure that the curbs of the garden areas are almost imperceptible and the gravel and grass define the boundaries.

0195 A leak in an underground parking lot was the cause of the renovation of Malvern City Square in Melbourne, Australia, designed by Rush Wright Associates. For the steps, ramps and retaining walls, and anti-slip granite was used.

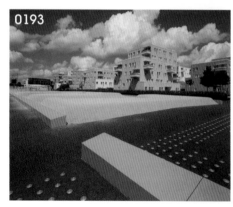

0196

Section

0196 One of the highlights of Union Point Park, designed by the studio led by Mario Schjetnan, GDU, is a pergola that provides shade and a place to rest and have a picnic.

0197 Curbs, walkways, large decorative boulders and other elements make up the boundaries of the city square next to the water in Sjövikstorget, a work by Sweco Architects. These elements also delineate points of interest or reference for citizens.

0198 For the Promenade Pierre, Sweco architects considered a review of eighteenth century Japanese gardens. The design features a line with curbs of the same material, which separates the space in two.

0199 For the bathing area of Spain's Barcelona Forum, Beth Galí designed several ways to access the water. In this case, she used steps so that users can go into the water or just sit and cool their feet.

0197

0198

0199

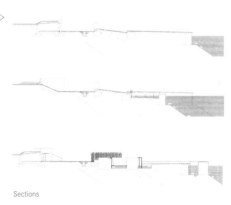

Sections

0200 The different models of curbs used in Thorndorn Park, designed by Oxigen, create two different types of landscapes, a water channel and an amphitheater, among the tidy lawns.

0201 A Plot-Megaron is a work to honor the deceased amid the hustle and bustle of the city. This SLA project consists of 30 lots of grass or sandstone in the form of steps.

0202 Jean Max Llorca, of JML Consultants, designed wooden banks for the closed circuit of water for the Blanc-Mesnil Water Square, France. The aim was to create a warm space for citizens.

0203 The construction of two buildings on Graadt van Roggernweg Street in Utrech left an undeveloped lot, which was used for this garden, designed by Delta Vorm Groep. The steps and curbs are in charge of defining the space occupied by box hedges.

0204 In Punta Pite, Chile, a project was carried out that combines 29 lots located in rugged terrain. The project, by Estudio del Paisaje Teresa Moller & Asociados, links the spaces with a few steps fully integrated into the land that convert the landscape into visual poetry.

0205 ASPECT Studios was commissioned to design the Wetland 5 Park. Part of the banks of the lake has been urbanized so that large stone blocks form a sort of amphitheater facing the water.

0206 Gualtiero Oberti used cement colored with metal oxides for different elements, including benches, low walls and dividers, for the Cunella Riverside Park. The design was based on nature and mathematics.

0207 In a parkland project on a site formerly owned by BP, McGregor Coxall has used various architectural elements, such as stairs, ramps and walkways, to integrate areas that for 60 years were the home of 31 tanks of mineral oil.

0200

0201

0202

0203

0204

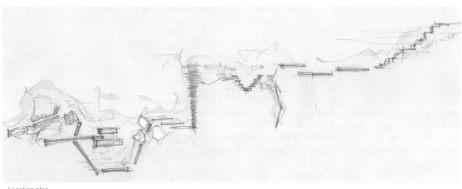

Location plan

0205

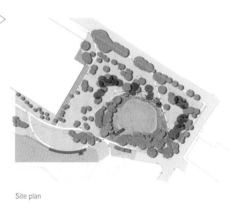

Site plan

0206

0207

0208 The different designs of the steps of the Nueva School campus adapt to the needs of each space: at times they are more regular, and at other times they are extended and form benches and sloping spaces.

0209 Although the construction of some architectural elements, such as stairs or curbs, is usually carried out with prefabricated pieces, these can also be custom designed with materials such as concrete, thus allowing them to be adapted to specific needs.

0210 The Battery Park City Streetscape project is located southwest of Manhattan, New York. This design by Paolo Bürgi uses materials and light to reinforce the linear nature of the path. The pergola reinforces the effect of light and transmits a sense of lightness.

0211 One of the entrances to the University of Pittsburgh, designed by Payette Associates, is characterized by the concrete paving and the dark and polished stone of the sides of the flower beds that direct visitors to the interior of the enclosure.

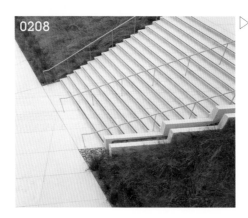

Axonometry

Plan of the access area

0212 The Split House, by Atelier Feichang Jianzhu, is divided into two volumes. The steps have been positioned in the space between these volumes. As well as permitting the designers to avoid modifying the land, these steps connect the various levels, providing access to the house and forming the tree pits.

0213 In this Turnbull Griffin Haesloop project, mobile elements have been used, including metal sheets and wooden pallets, to bridge the gap between the Sebastopol residence and the owner's studio.

0214 With their renovation of Rue Pams, Michele & Miquel Architectes & Paysagistes adapted the space to the needs of the current population by building two levels of steps. The first has the usual dimensions, and in the second the steps almost disappear and turn into a ramp.

0215 The Storaa Stream project, by Okra Landschapsarchitecten, has become the center of Holstebr, Denmark, connecting two areas of the city. The public space has been transformed into an outdoor stage by elements such as steps that become stands.

0216 Although primarily decorative, these fences on a landfill site in the region of Garraf, in Catalonia, serve to rearrange circulation on the land, which, after the landfill was closed was restored by architects Batlle i Roig.

0217 For Brandt Landskap, it is best to consider the initial requirements of a project as a challenge and an opportunity to develop new solutions rather than as an obstacle.

0218 In the St. Anne Veterans Hospital by Cardinal Hardy, there are several gardens designed to assist in the recovery of individual patients. The fences, lighting and street furniture have been designed for this purpose.

0219 For Bureau B+B, the best compliment a project can receive is to trigger the curiosity of visitors. The project Looking for Jane, in Makeblijde, the Netherlands, in which a portion of the fence opens to let visitors pass to the other side, meets this criteria.

0220 With the design of the fences of one of the Aalborg, Denmark, waterfront areas, a project by C. F. Møller, two goals are accomplished: pedestrians are protected and, thanks to the different heights, benches for rest areas are created.

0221 The materials chosen for the Aalborg waterfront project, are as harsh and rough as the fjord itself. Corten steel has been selected for the fences that protect one of the sets of steps of this major town planning project.

0222 The fence in this space, designed by Gerhard Rennhofer, surrounds the complex and, despite its low height, separates the different areas. In addition, it merges with the wooden street furniture.

0223 The quality of a landscape project lies both in its general design process and the attention to detail, like in this Beukplein fence. Carve architects designed it in collaboration with the neighbors and achieved a bigger and more accessible space.

0216

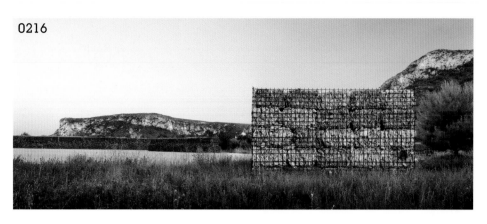

0217

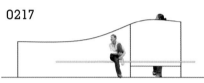

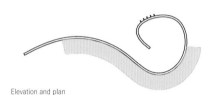

Elevation and plan

0218

0219

0220

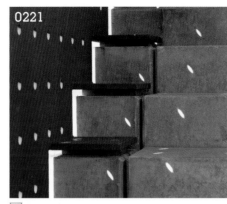

0221

▽

0222

0223

0224 The Johansson Landskab studio attempts to create something unique in each project, regardless of the budget or size. In this small playground, measurements have been adapted to kids, and the fences dividing the areas are low-lying.

0225 The Johansson Landskab landscape draws inspiration from childhood and then recreates the sensations experienced in parks and gardens. In this proposal, a low stone fence and another surrounding the more remote play area stand out.

0226 The fence that separates the area where there is a stone bench from the sloping garden has been built with glass. The transparency of the material allows the spatial continuity of the project, designed by the Japanese firm Earthscape.

0227 For Gustafson Porter, adapting the materials to the landscape can unify color, texture, shape and movement. In this path, fenced with simple branches, the sensation of nature is conveyed despite the intervention of humans.

0224

0225

0227

0226

0228 The landscape surrounding architectural projects is often the source of inspiration for Landskap Design architects. The mountains surrounding the city were the inspiration for the granite stone walls of the Bergen Festival Square in Norway.

0229 History is another element to consider when designing urban spaces. The funicular square designed by Landskap Design recovers and reinterprets the Art Nouveau aesthetic of the original building on the stone wall surrounding the space.

0230 The use of expensive materials does not result in better design and outcome. These concrete walls designed by McGregor Coxall demarcate a path while creating an open space with straight lines.

0231 Architect María Teresa Cervantes chose logs for the fence that surrounds the remains of this tomb. The choice came after a study of the light, colors and textures of the environment.

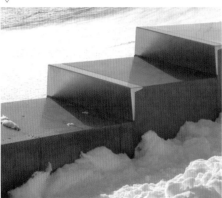

0232 The Raglan Street Parkland fence, the work of Site Office Landscape Architecture, defines the urban area next to a road, absorbs traffic noise and gives visual continuity to the park.

0233 In this private garden, Shades of Green architects mix the gray tones of the floor with the red wall and wooden fence. The combination of warm and cool colors becomes another design element.

0234 The delicacy of some of the materials used to build fences, such as bamboo or plants, can create a pleasant atmosphere. This is more common in the gardens of private homes, as in this outdoor space designed by N-tree.

0235 Bollards are landscape features that prevent vehicles from invading pedestrian areas. In the Oerliker Park, designed by Schweingruber Zulauf, the bollards on both sides of the street safeguard pedestrians.

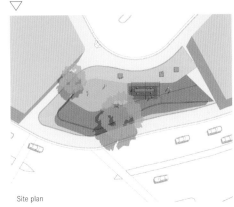

Site plan

0236 The architects at Shades of Green Landscape Architecture believe that the exterior should be well lit, especially the small backyards common in urban homes. Here they have designed a private yard with an original translucent glass fence that allows the passage of light.

0237 Strootman Landschapsarchitecten has designed an original fence for the Eusebiushof building, which is completed with customized wheelbarrows that can be used as seats. When in their place, the wheelbarrows close off access to the lawn.

0238 Among the materials that form the fences that surround the Redding residence, by Kendle Design Collaborative, the rammed earth and Corten steel stand out.

0239 This fence, located at Tanner Springs Park designed by Atelier Dreiseitl, has been built with some old railroad tracks, paying tribute to the industrial past of the city.

0240 A 229-foot (70 m) Corten steel fence surrounds the courtyard of the Nicolai Cultural Center, designed by Kristine Jensen Landscapearchitect, framing an area designed for citizen participation.

0241 Kuhn Truninger designed the extension to the Weiach cemetery, respecting the former complex. The cemetery can be seen through the 6¹/₂-foot (2 m) larch wood slat fence.

Site plan

0242 Simple metal tubes form the fence surrounding the garden of the Scoon Residence, by the Kendle Design Collaborative architects. This fence keeps animals out without breaking continuity with the landscape.

0243 This design by Rockhill and Associates for the sustainable residential complex Lolomax incorporates repetitive elements, such as metal fences, to give uniformity to the complex.

0244 The restoration of Rue Pams, carried out by Michele & Miquel Architectes & Paysagistes, includes stairs and a fence composed of stone in the bottom half and a metal grille in the upper half, allowing the passage of air and providing visual continuity.

0245 The architects of the Hotel Tierra Atacama in Chile, Matías González and Rodrigo Searle, are committed to environmental sustainability and have used the rammed-earth technique for the fences surrounding the grounds, among other elements.

0246 To preserve the volcanic landscape of Bosc de Tosca, Spain, RCR Aranda Pigem Vilalta Arquitectes opted for Corten steel fences with half-open slats, which turn this park into an individual and rough landscape.

0247 The guardrail of this geological observatory, designed by Paolo Bürgi, fulfills two functions: to define the space and to protect visitors. Its lightweight design does not interrupt the view of the landscape. Each of the points of interest is identified on the guardrail.

0248 Sometimes the more traditional design is the best option and the one that allows residents to enjoy the natural elements. The guardrail that runs along the terrace of this private home, designed by Paolo Bürgi, integrates into the landscape thanks to its simplicity.

0249 Guardrails are indispensable elements in many public spaces. The design must conform to strict safety rules, such as height, materials, space between bars, etc. This lookout in Card, Switzerland, designed by Paolo Bürgi, is functional and adapts to the space.

0247

0248

0249

0250

0251

0252

0253

0254

0250 These simple guardrails, designed by Cardinal Hardy for the exterior areas of St. Anne Veterans Hospital in Montreal, Canada, demarcate the gardens that revitalize the entrance to the building.

0251 The Melis Stokepar by Carve, a playground in a park, has been created based on the demands of users and is intended to meet their needs without neglecting security. The bars of the guardrails join together or separate according to the curve forming the path of the upper area.

0252 A simple guardrail marks the farthest limit of a series of terraces, secured to the ground with gabions, in the Vredenburg Reserve, South Africa, designed by Habitat Landscape Architects. On this occasion, the guardrail is a visual element that defines the boundaries of a landscape created by humans.

0253 This trail designed by Paolo Bürgi crosses through a bamboo forest and ends at a small lookout that penetrates into the space. This has been protected with a high guardrail and features a small seat at which to stop off along the way and enjoy the feeling of being surrounded by nature.

0254 For Gerhard Rennhofer, materials are part of the functional structure of a project. Therefore, the wrought iron of the guardrail is suitable for outdoor areas and ages well, enriching the final result.

0255 Jos van de Lindeloof wanted to give continuity to the landscape and has installed a guardrail with steel cables onto this small bridge — equally safe but less visible.

0256 The Nerang Bridge in Canberra, Australia, works as both a bridge and as a lookout for Lake Burley Griffin. In the opinion of Oxigen architects, it is important to take into account the community's opinion in the design of a project.

0257 The central location of the guardrail of these steps in the outdoor areas of the Willamette National Cemetery, Oregon, the work of Mayer/Reed, divides the steps in two and strengthens their sinuous lines.

0258 For this pedestrian bridge over a pond at the entrance of an office building on Adelaide Street in Toronto, Canada, Janet Rosenberg proposes robust and metallic guardrails that can be used as benches.

0259 The materials used in protective elements such as fences and guardrails are diverse and adapted to the aesthetic chosen by the architects. These metal railings on the Eastbank Esplanade in Oregon, by Mayer/Reed, maintain the industrial aesthetic of the area.

0260

0260 The roof of the International Port Terminal in Yokohama, Japan, by Foreign Office Architects, simulates a futuristic landscape of artificial dunes. Stainless-steel and wire-mesh guardrails were installed on iroko wood.

0261 In densely populated cities it is increasingly important to open and create space for citizens, such as the Eastbank Esplanade in Oregon, a work by Mayer/Reed. Safety features like guardrails are essential for waterfront spaces.

0262 The Rain Garden, by Mayer/Reed, at the Oregon Convention Center was built to show how the vegetation could recover and filter rainwater. The guardrail on the footbridge over the water circuit explains the project.

0263 The Rotermann Quarter project, by Oü Ab Kosmos, pays tribute to the area's industrial past. In the space between two buildings, the metal pipe guardrails and steel surfaces that clad the walls stand out.

0264 The Lucien Rose residential complex, designed by Atelier du Pont, integrates the different blocks of social housing with the outdoor spaces. Functional guardrails demarcate the pedestrian spaces and the boundaries of the site.

0265 For the bridge over the Storaen River, Tegnestuen Schul Landskabarkitekter studio chose railings that illuminate the path during the long winter nights.

0266 The renovation of historic gardens combines past and future, both in the approach and in the details. Birk Nielsen of Sweco Architects has prioritized the historical aspect of this garden, as can be seen with the choice of guardrails.

0267 The platform on the wetlands in the Shanghai Houtan Park, designed by Turenscape, has a simple guardrail that highlights the natural landscape.

0268 This pedestrian walkway connects the Vltava River with Prague Castle in the Czech Republic. Architect Josef Pleskot, from AP Atelier, designed a route that passes through nature and causes little impact on the ecosystem. A simple wooden bridge and metal guardrails form the outdoor trails.

0269 Infrastructure can also become landscape, such as the guardrails of the Zhongshan Shipyard Park, China, designed by Turenscape architects.

0270

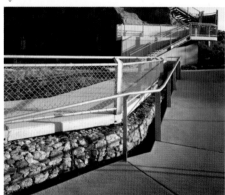

0271

0272

0273

0270 The cost of materials and maintenance can tip the balance when designing an outdoor space. For this reason, McGregor Coxall chose galvanized steel for the guardrails of the parkland on a site formerly owned by BP.

0271 The Valmuy Pathway, by Feichtinger Architectes, is 288 feet (88 m) long, 14³/₄ feet (4.5 m) wide and has a height between 20 and 26 feet (6–8 m) above street level. The main materials are steel and glass for the wind protection screens.

0272 This viewing platform designed by Jensen & Skodvin Arkitektkontor stands out for the curves that adapt to the morphology of the terrain. The guardrails that curve inward allow visitors to peer into the water-falls safely.

0273 oslund.and.assoc. have designed a simple space under the I35W bridge on the Mississippi River. Both the plants and the architectural elements are simple: plants that require little maintenance, simple metal guardrails, concrete floor and stone gabions for the terraces that bridge the gap.

0274 The railway line passing through Graz, Austria, has 13 underpasses. 3:0 Landschaftsarchitektur architects were commissioned to organize the movement of vehicles and the separation of elements. The terraces are separated by walls and the cycle lane with a high security railing.

0275 Okra Landschapsarchitecten is responsible for the Afrikaanderplein project. The fence surrounding the park area provides security, sustainability and quality of use. During the day, the 98-foot (30 m) railings fully open up, providing easy access.

0276 The selection of plants is one of the key elements when defining the identity of a landscape. To achieve a better visual effect in the Pflegi-Areal project in Switzerland, Schweingruber Zulauf designers have surrounded the trunks with a grille filled with stones.

0277 Tejo Remy & René Veenhuizen, the designers of these original railings for a school playground, tried to integrate them into the children's games so they would not be considered a barrier to the outside world.

0278 Bjørbekk & Lindheim Architects have redesigned outdoor spaces in the new Rolfsbukta neighborhood in Fornebu, Norway. In addition to a new boardwalk, the water has penetrated interior spaces to provide an air of originality to the landscape.

0279 C+S architects designed this wooden platform for the entrance to the 60th Venice Film Festival. The shape of the platform represents waves that, in turn, symbolize the movie stars, whose fame, success and money comes and goes.

0280 The design of this boardwalk, by Brandt Land-skab, focuses on attention to detail despite the large size of the project. The mixture of materials enriches the space and visually separates the walkways.

0281 Cardinal Hardy architects placed wooden plat-forms on the lawns surrounding these residential buildings, which are easily integrated into the outdoor spaces and lead the way to the street.

0278

0279

0280

0281

0282 Jos van de Lindeloof works on his projects with the idea that contrast creates tension and generates new landscapes. The wooden platforms and pond between the buildings create a natural corner amidst urban architecture.

0283 In the Melis Stokepark project, located in the Hague, the Netherlands, and designed by Carve, the wooden slats of the circuit platform add the finishing touches and make this playground stand out.

0284 This circular pond, designed by Earthscape, is situated on an elegant deck of wooden slats. A concrete walkway runs through the feature.

0285

0286

0285 According to Francis Landscapes, creating space for terraces and roofs is losing importance. It is necessary to regenerate these outdoor spaces and build them verticality. A pond and a wooden platform have been added to this private terrace, recreating a more natural environment.

0286 The way Ilias Lolidis, the creator of this residence, designed this space gives prominence to the materials in the outdoor areas. In this way, the beauty and texture of the materials, such as the wooden slats that surround the pool, is better appreciated.

0287

0288

▽

0289

0290

0291

0287 During the design process, an initial concept could end up being transformed into something more tangible. In this work by Johansson Landskab, the colored seats appear to emerge from the wooden platform itself.

0288 For Johansson Landskab, it is important to use experiences in the design of outdoor spaces. These circular wooden platforms are reminders of children's games in the woods.

0289 The design by C. F. Møller for the waterfront in Aalborg, Denmark, includes a study of the lighting necessary to give character to this area and to ensure proper lighting during the winter season when there are fewer hours of sunshine.

0290 LAND-I is a landscape architecture studio that is characterized by its bold projects and artistic proposals. Wooden slats form a sort of circular platform in that famous installation, Mente-la-Menta? (mind the mint?).

0291 These structures designed by LAND-I, consisting of a wooden platform and a lightweight roof, are distributed around the outdoor areas of a yoga retreat center as experimental work elements.

0292 A small wooden slatted platform is the spot chosen by Mayer/Reed to place benches and create a place of rest for workers in the PDX building.

0293 In this pergola by Scape Design Associates, the use of wood stands out. Waterproof timber, whether through some kind of treatment or because of its tropical origin, is suitable for platforms surrounding wet areas such as swimming pools.

0294 Strootman Landschapsarchitecten seeks to merge architecture and landscape when designing the landscape of residential areas. In the Bloemendalerpolder project, east of Amsterdam, the Netherlands, platforms and paths along the water channels are included.

0295 In this garden designed by N-tree, a platform of wooden slats is used to separate levels and an outdoor dining area from an area with more abundant vegetation, which creates a more contemplative atmosphere.

0296 The reasons for the success of this SWA project, the Gubei pathway in Shanghai, China, are innovation, design and research in the choice of native vegetation. A striking wooden platform is one of the highlights of the project.

0297 Landscape architects can help cities become more resilient and adapt to changing infrastructure and the effects of climate change. In the Cedar Rapids project, Sasaki architects propose lightweight platforms to facilitate access to people.

0298 Simon Rackham sought ideas to transform the courtyard of a home into a space for children, adults and vegetation. A wooden platform is the simplest and cheapest solution to connect the different levels and divide uses.

0299 People tend to converge around the boundaries of plazas. In Sjövikstorget, Stockholm, Thorbjörn Andersson of Sweco Architects has converted the ends of two long boardwalks that frame the boundaries of the plaza.

0294

Photomontage

0295

0296

0297

Photomontage

0298

0299

0300 Thomas Balsley Associates studio addresses their designs by gathering local knowledge and knowledge of the social environment. In the Curtis Hixon Park, platforms have been installed that suggest the routes, but it is the users who decide if they use them as walkways or children's play areas.

0301 In the Shanghai Houtan Park, designed by Turenscape, the presence of plants that filter the water is combined with a few walkways that allow the community to enjoy this landscape.

0302 Trees signal the end of a platform of wooden slats designed by Verdier. The tree area has been created to relieve a possible excess of architectural forms.

0303 Thorbjörn Andersson from Sweco Architects takes into account the different times of day to design a landscape. The walkway next to the river in the Sandgrund Park in the Swedish town of Karlstad takes advantage of major changes in light for a particularly pleasant experience at sunset.

0300

0301

0302

0303

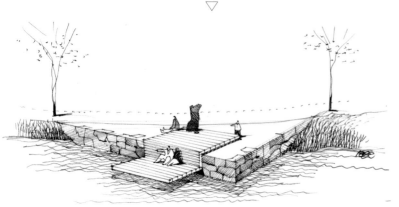
Sketch

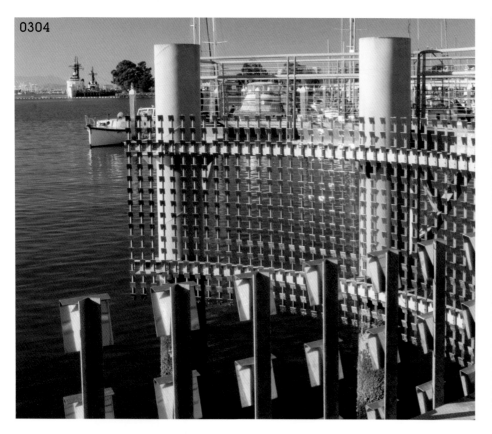

0304

0305

0304 In its first project in the United States, Mario Schjetnans's studio created walkways and lookouts along the old docks in Oakland, California. The beneficiaries were the children of the districts of Fruitvale and San Antonio, who were in need of recreational space.

0305 The renovation of the Camino de Ronda de S'Agaró, by RGA Arquitectes, has restored a boardwalk with a long history. The Camí de Ronda, an ancient patrol route of the Costa Brava in Catalonia, has become a tourist route along the Catalan coast.

0306 The Vinaròs micro-coast project, designed by Guallart Architects, consists of small island-shaped platforms that facilitate the access and enjoyment of the rocky area of this part of the Valencian coast, Spain.

0307 ASPECT Studios designed the new park at the site of the former headquarters of Sydney's Water Police. It uses precast concrete slabs to form steps and platforms at varying levels to reinforce the experience of tidal water movements. The area is a dynamic urban waterfront boardwalk with piers and rest areas.

0306

0307

Perspective

0308

0309

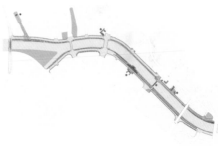

Site plan

0310

0308 The elevated and winding layout of the wooden deck of the youth center in Copenhagen, Denmark, designed by PLOT=BIG+JDS, allows the mooring of vessels in the bottom and creates an area for young people to play.

0309 This project addresses the renovation of 12 miles (20 km) of shoreline along the Hai River as it passes through Tianjin, China. EDAW architects were able to take advantage of the gap between the roadway and the channel to create a riverside walk that is open to pedestrians and closed to traffic.

0310 The urban project of Las Margas in the Spanish Pyrenees, designed by Verzone Woods Architectes, boasts artificial water reserves among roads, pathways along the water's edge, ramps and steps.

0311 This pier, designed by Thorbjörn Andersson from Sweco Architects, is located in Sandgrund Park in Sweden. An item as simple as this can transform an empty space into an evocative and poetic landscape.

0312 The renovation that the Landlab architects have carried out on this old port in the center of the city of Almere in the Netherlands has restored the public space. In addition to the dock and a slipway, a walkway was built along the water.

0311

0312

0313 The initial draft of this waterfront zone includes a beach along the promenade. Finally in the end, Brandt Landskab replaced it with a sun terrace, which gave the end space more visual power.

0314 Landscape architecture transforms outdoor areas into spaces brimming with life. For Brandt Landskab, it is the design components, rather than the visiting public, that transform and revitalize an area, as a public space can be beautiful, regardless of whether it is popular or not.

0315 This pathway built in Aalborg, Denmark, next to the fjord is composed of various materials and elements. The architects at C. F. Møller have included some elevated platforms from which people can enjoy the industrial landscape.

0316 The Red Bridge is a project by 1/1 Architecture designed for Izmit Bay, Turkey, which reaches the Sea of Marmara thanks to an artificial lake. This bridge is an ecological proposal for a riverside area in a neighborhood.

0317 The extension of the coastal area from Bondi to Bronte, Australia, is a design by ASPECT Studios that simply and subtly reveals the complexity and fullness of the coastal landscape.

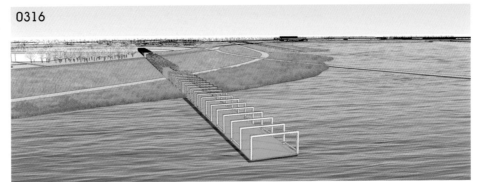

Sketch

Sketch

0318

0319

0320

0321

0322

0323

0318 This park bridge in Llobregat, Spain, has been built to facilitate movement around the natural space. Batlle i Roig architects designed the routes to inform visitors' personal perception and knowledge.

0319 This park has a dynamic mix of uses: a walkway has been designed that also serves as a covered bridge over the artificial lake.

0320 A decorative concrete bridge allows visitors to cross this small pond designed by Earthscape. The words relating to the sky and sea complete this poetic image.

0321 Batlle i Roig architects believe that landscape work must adapt to the vegetation and nature and not vice versa. In Las Llamas, in Santander, Spain, transit areas have been built on wetlands while still protecting the ecosystem.

0322 In the yard of this private home, Francis Landscapes has designed a hideaway amidst nature. Vegetation and water surround this small pergola, which can be accessed by a concrete walkway.

0323 The work by Gora Art & Landscape enhances the beauty and the landscape. These two lookouts are spots from which to contemplate the landscape and give you a feeling of sailing through the air.

0324 This bridge with wooden slats and recessed lighting, by Ioakim-Loizas, has been designed as a footbridge from which to enjoy and view the park activities at your feet.

0325 On many occasions, observing nature offers the solution to how to approach a landscape project. This bridge by Jos van de Lindeloof merges with the environment and recreates a bucolic landscape.

0326 Jos van de Lindeloof bases the design of architectural elements on the role assigned by the users, preventing disproportionate solutions to simple needs. This bridge is an example of design in keeping with need.

0327 For MADE associati, it is important to consider the reuse and reinvention of abandoned landscapes that harbor great potential and may once again be an active part of the environment.

0328 The landscape design and the landscape itself are complementary. If the second adapts to the first, nature will appropriate the artificial elements, such as this Jos van de Lindeloof bridge, which becomes part of the natural landscape.

Photomontage

0329

0329 KLA has built this bridge with a single stone measuring 16¹/₂ x 6¹/₂ feet (5 x 2 m). For the rail, rope and wood has been used. The use of local materials has ensured that the bridge fits into the landscape.

0330 Generating spaces that people care about creates a sense of community. To design attractive spaces for people, according to Mayer/Reed, the spaces should reflect the values and history and contribute to a quality of life for the population.

0331 Water can be used in various ways, and bridges that pass over rivers, lakes or wetlands should be adapted to fuse function and aesthetics. Concrete slabs on wooden rails designed by Jos van de Lindeloof form a simple, eye-catching bridge.

0330

0331

0332 The renewal of the Willamette River generated the Eastbank Esplanade in Oregon. Mayer/Reed architects created a space where bridges and walkways give importance to pedestrians and to the connection with alternative transportation.

0333 When Rehwaldt Landschaftsarchitekten design a park they create a green space in the city. These spaces include furniture, bridges and other items that indicate the depth and direction of the space.

0334 Ecology defines the Kunming Eco-Communities project, by SWA Group, so it works within the ecosystem of pine forests, ravines and wetlands. As an example, the green spaces have been maintained and protected with walkways and an old pond has been recovered.

0335 The recreational areas designed by Rehwaldt Landschaftsarchitekten are dream landscapes. From the vegetation and other elements, such as bridges, games, tables and benches, spaces that let your imagination run free, especially for children, are generated.

0336 The design of this walkway in Vallparadís Park in Barcelona, Spain, by RGA Arquitectes, shows how technology may add elements to the landscape without destroying its essence. The simplicity of design enhances the aesthetics of the park.

0337 The Nieuwe Hollandse Waterline, which is nearly 53 miles (85 km) long, has breaks along it in places that generate truly poetic spaces. Okra Landschapsarchitecten has designed this bridge that leads from the break in the defense space to the channel.

0338 In the recovery of the banks of the River IJssel, the Netherlands, Okra Landschapsarchitecten studio installed pedestrian and cyclist bridges that stand out as they connect the river with the old part of the town.

0339 Rankinfraser Landscape Architecture works with all levels of a landscape: geological, historical, etc. In this case, the spaces have been created under the freeway, including walkways, an underpass and a bridge.

0340 Thorbjörn Andersson, of Sweco Architects studio, has maintained the industrial, heritage landscape in the Holmens Bruk, in the Norwegian town of Norrkoping. Some old oil containers and a slotted floor form this bridge with views of a waterfall.

0341 Okra Landschapsarchitecten has transformed the riverside into an open-air theater where the walkways, circuits and rest areas surround the cultural buildings. The bridge takes a central position and joins the two centers, each one located on a riverbank.

0336

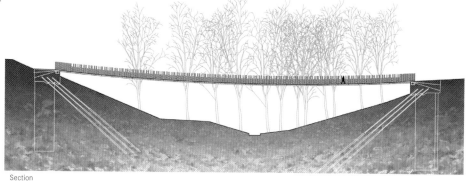

Section

0337

0338

0339

0340

0341

Holmens Bruk
Passage vid stålcylinder
Vy från kabelbron

Sketch

0342

0343

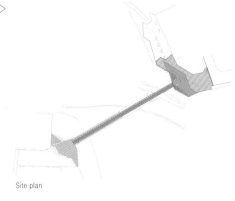

Site plan

0344

0345

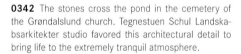

0342 The stones cross the pond in the cemetery of the Grøndalslund church. Tegnestuen Schul Landskabsarkitekter studio favored this architectural detail to bring life to the extremely tranquil atmosphere.

0343 Xavier Font Solà is responsible for the restoration of Pont Trencat in Sant Celoni, Spain. The bridge, destroyed in the Napoleonic wars, was not recovered until nearly two centuries later. An archaeological restoration underlines the differences between original and new.

0344 The Simone de Beauvoir pedestrian bridge, by Feichtinger Architectes, joins the National Library of France with Bercy Park. The compression and tension of the two arches that form the bridge allow a clear span of 636 feet (194 m) and improve circulation options.

0345 Gudbrandsjuvet pedestrian bridges, by Jensen & Skodvin Arkitektkontor, comprises several zigzag platforms. Its main construction consists of three wires soldered to the posts on both sides of the bridges and guided to each of the foundations.

0346

0347

0348

0349

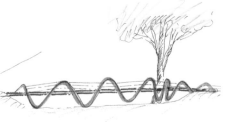

Sketch

0346 This fantastic footbridge over a highway, a construction by Taylor Cullity Lethlean, manages to break the monotony of these roads. The Corten steel plates and the semicircular form stand out.

0347 The shoreline park of Dania, in Malmö, Sweden, offers magnificent views of the Strait of Öresund. Thorbjörn Andersson, from Sweco Architects, provides different ways to enjoy the sea, among which this lookout is a prominent feature.

0348 Okra architects were responsible for the reintegration of the Melaan channel to the historic Belgian city of Mechelen. Water was returned to the dry riverbed, and a series of bridges that connect the ends were built, recovering its lost charm.

0349 Terragram (now Room 4.1.3) architects joined forces with Aston Raggat Mcdougall to design the National Museum of Australia. The bridge of the Australian Garden of Dreams is one of the main elements.

0350 West 8 has converted the former industrial area of Kanaaleiland in an area of public spaces with a network of paths for cyclists and pedestrians. The bridges, strategically located, provide a new identity to the site while connecting the area with the city.

0351 The Twist, a bridge in Vlaardingen, is an important link in the bike lane network in the Dutch province of South Holland and forms an urban route that connects with the Broekpolder. The form and color of the bridge give the area an identity.

0352 The dyed-red guindo walkway highlights the personality of this magnificent project that uses the thermal springs of the Villarrica National Park in the Andes. The progression of the Germán del Sol structure includes terraces from which to enjoy the landscape.

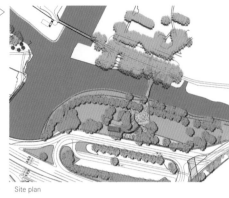

Site plan

3-D representation

0353

0353 The memory of a boundless landscape inspired Juan Antonio Sánchez, from Adhoc MSL, to design the cantilever walkway in Alto de Bayna. To achieve the feeling of levitation, he designed a structure of gold-colored steel sheets that matches the colors of the environment.

0354 Carl-Viggo Hølmebakk built a bridge between a dense pine forest overlooking the lake and mountains that recalls the view of this same landscape by the Norwegian painter Harald Sohlberg. Note that the concrete structure has not caused any damage to the trees or their root system.

0355 Felipe Peña Pereda and Francisco Novoa Rodríguez are responsible for the Ethnographic Park of Insúa. The steel remains from the original structure have been used for the lookout that penetrates into the sea. The project gives continuity to the use of the coastline.

0354

0355

Section

0356 Architects Todd Saunders and Tommie Wilhelmsen were responsible for the design of this lookout for the Sogn of Fjordane fjord in Aurland, Norway. A pine structure invites the visitor to peer into the depths of the fjord, and it is topped with a tempered glass protective sheet that lets you better enjoy the views.

0357 The objective of 3LHD architects was to provide a functional element with a monumental character. The result is a highly symbolic memorial bridge with tactile qualities that balances the horizontal nature of the vertical monolithic pillars.

0358 The Brick Pit Ring, by Durbach Block Architects, is an aerial walkway that has become a lookout and a sort of elevated plaza that allows you to enjoy the landscape where a quarry was once located, the last trace of the industrial past of the area.

0356

0357

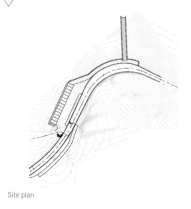

Site plan

0358

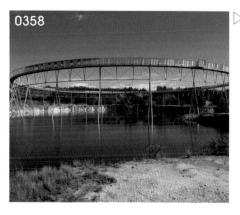

Site plan

0359

Construction diagram

0360

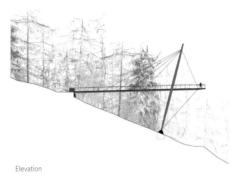

Elevation

0361

0362

0359 The Anyang Peak lookout tower, designed by the prestigious MVRDV studio, captures the charm of Anyang Recreational Park. The tower, which stands out for its curved lines, covers 479 feet (146 m) and reaches 49 feet (15 m) in height.

0360 Paolo Bürgi integrated the promontory, which in reality is a path that seems to be suspended in the air, into the Cardada Mountain. This element crosses the forest and, at the end of the path, reveals the lookout from which to contemplate the sweeping landscape.

0361 This bird observatory designed by 70°N Arkitektur consists of two 21^1/$_4$-foot (6.5 m) high towers. The lookouts have a simple structure, a steel base and lined with wood, but are resistant to strong winds.

0362 The exteriors of the General Mills Corporation, by oslund.and.assoc., aims to be a pleasant space and follow the modern aesthetic of the surrounding buildings. The pools of water with the bridges and green areas accentuate the geometry of the landscape and create a relaxed atmosphere.

0363

0364

0365

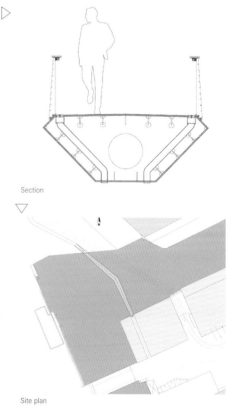

Section

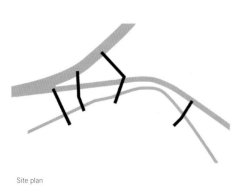

Site plan

Site plan

0366

0367

0368

0368

0369

0363 Broekbakema is responsible for this pedestrian bridge with curved lines located in the interior courtyard of the Shell International Exploration and Production building in Rijswijk, the Netherlands.

0364 Mangfallpark is an urban park created following the transfer of an industrial area to another part of the city. A24 Landschaft studio has designed a series of walkways and pedestrian bridges to facilitate movement through these natural spaces near the urban core.

0365 This simple walkway designed by Feichtinger Architectes connects the museum building with the rest of the city. The two sections of the facing inclination that form it prevent the use of pillars.

0366 This footbridge winds 295 feet (90 m) through the dense urban fabric of the business district of La Défense, Paris, France. The structure of the footbridge maintains its rigidity thanks to a series of architectural elements that work as the skeleton.

0367 The footbridges located over the channels in Strasbourg, France, are defined by the urban environment. The industrial aspect of the previous uses is toned down with this renovation by Feichtinger Architectes, which softens the lines and invites tranquility and leisure.

0368 This pedestrian footbridge with a bike lane over the River Rin, by Feichtinger Architectes, joins the banks of two countries: France and Germany. In addition, it is a few feet from the border these countries share with Switzerland.

0369 The Kul Kul Bridge is in the Green School complex, a sustainable campus designed by PT Bambu. The buildings, all built with sustainable, technical materials, are located on both banks of the River Ayung, in Sibang Kaja, Bali.

0370 Vo Trong Nghia is a Vietnamese architect who combines modern architectural aesthetics with traditional, technical materials. In his bar and restaurant projects, such as the wNw café and bar and the Flamingo club, he incorporates bridges over water and bamboo decks.

0371 The Monument in the Lake Lausitz by Architektur und Landschaft is a stunning lookout of Corten steel that rises 98 feet (30 m) above the ground. From the top, hills covered with pine trees and meadows can be seen. This landscape will be completed in the future with water that will flood abandoned mines.

0372 The bamboo bridge in the Soneva Kiri holiday resort in Thailand, by Jorg Stamm, leads visitors to the main installations. This engineering structure was designed as a large-scale structure and is 98 feet (30 m) long.

0370

0371

Sketch

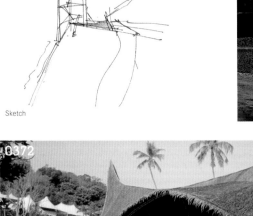

0372

0373

Sketch

0374

0376

0376

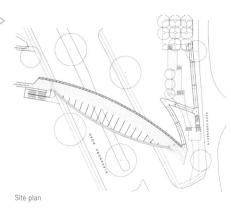

Site plan

0377

0378

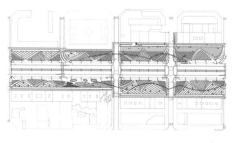

Site plan

0373 The High Line was an elevated subway line in New York City that fell into disuse in 1980. A people's initiative managed to achieve its restoration as a public park of walkways and bridges. James Corner Field Operations and Diller Scofidio + Renfro were responsible for the work.

0374 The Forest Walk, by Look Architects, is a galvanized steel structure throughout the forest close to the city of Singapore that brings nature closer to the urban area. This footbridge is between 10 and 60 feet (3–18 m) off the ground and is 5 1/4 feet (1.6 m) long.

0375 Landscape architect Jos van de Lindeloof has created a small wooden bridge hidden among the lush vegetation of this private garden. The aim was to merge the architectural elements among the foliage to enhance nature.

0376 In the same park in Singapore, the studio Look Architects designed the Alexandra Arch, a bridge over 20 feet (6 m) in height at the end of the walkway that goes from Telok Blangah Hill to Alexandra Road.

0377 Birk Nielsen, from Sweco Architects, has been inspired by the design of the garden of a historic castle. By adapting the new architectural features to the existing ones, consistency is achieved throughout the complex.

0378 The renovation of Gran Vía in Barcelona, Spain, is used to increase the number of pedestrian bridges that cross this infrastructure. Arriola & Fiol architects pursued a landscape improvement for the whole complex and managed to improve neighborhood connections.

0379

0380

0381

0382

▽

0383

0379 The Torvdalshalsen rest area in Norway designed by 70°N Arkitektur, minimizes the impact on nature. The seating areas are protected by a fence covered with dark panels that protect from the wind and store heat, creating a pleasant microclimate for users.

0380 When reflecting on a square or public garden, it is important to remember the people who will frequent this outdoor space: their ages, size, activities, etc. In Jacaranda Square, Australia, by ASPECT Studios, the customized benches adapt to this variety of users.

0381 The design should not dominate the landscape. ASPECT Studios have applied this maxim to the furniture with horizontal lines echoing the coast of Elwood in Melbourne, Australia. The main protagonists are the sea and horizon.

0382 Knowing the times and seasons when a public space will be used is important for its design. In this case, the benches of this walkway designed by Brandt Landskab can be used 7 days a week, 365 days a year.

0383 When the only reference is the sea and the tools available to interact with it are artificial, it is necessary to reinterpret nature. These benches designed by Beth Galí represent rocks from which to contemplate the sea at this bathing area.

0384 The TC Bohinj Park, Slovenia, by Bruto Landscape Architecture, includes a few simple benches made with wooden beams. The power of natural materials, such as solid wood, brings personality to the space.

0384

0385 In architectural design, intelligent solutions are always simple. Using modules in street furniture is one of them. The Pavilion Mobitel project, by Bruto Landscape Architecture, can combine and increase its surface area according to the customer's needs.

0386 Several elements designed by Burger Landschaftsarchitekten for this interior courtyard manage to reinforce the three-dimensionality of the space, one of the goals for this project. The concrete and reed benches serve as a guide for the tree branches.

0387 The port square in Kreuzlingen, Switzerland, represents the connection between the city and the landscape. The design by Paolo Bürgi incorporates seating from which to contemplate the horizon of the lake and the movement of ships.

0388 At Bureau B+B, they deem it necessary to know where each of the projects they undertake will be located. You can always find a hidden treasure that serves as inspiration for the final design, as in this children's area in Valkenberg Park.

0389 Norman Bethune Square, located on the campus of Concordia University in Montreal, Canada, has been reconfigured by Cardinal Hardy with the aim of creating a vibrant public space with benches and pedestrian zones, reducing traffic.

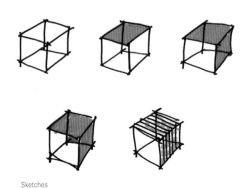

Sketches

0390

0391

0392

0393

0394

0390 According to Carve studio, it is important to gather ideas and views of both users and customers. It is the responsibility of the designer to improve the project concept if possible. Meerpark, in Amsterdam, the Netherlands, added public spaces for everyone rather than a space only to practice sports.

0391 The Aalborg promenade in Denmark, designed by C. F. Møller, creates a multitude of corners dedicated to space for relaxation, parks and places to rest where you are protected from traffic and wind.

0392 The Holla Wall project is a children's play structure that meets several requirements: a play area and climbing wall in a confined space at a low cost. Carve designers have managed to create a framework with space for 60 children.

0393 This stone bench is a thermometer-type structure designed by Earthscape. The color of the tiles means that they accumulate more or less heat during the year, making it better to sit on dark stones in winter and light colored stones in summer.

0394 For Gerhard Rennhofer, a good design is one that can be minimized while still having all the necessary qualities. This small courtyard is clearly demarcated, and the table and benches are the focal point.

0395 There is no reason why designing street furniture should be more expensive than other furniture. Idealice studio designed the benches for the Science Park in Linz, Austria, and integrated them into the architecture of the space, constructed by Caramel.

0396 The design of the lamps of the Science Park in Linz is another work by Idealice. To achieve a more resounding effect, it was considered necessary to design individual streetlamps that give strength to a design that attempts to transform the lines of the space.

0397 In the AHS Contiweg School, in Vienna, Austria, Idealice designers came up with a bench that also serves as a parking place for bicycles. In addition to customizing the environment, space is saved.

0397

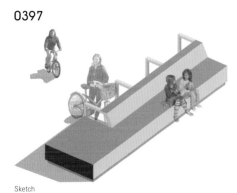

Sketch

0398

0399

0400

0398 For Jos van de Lindeloof, the design and landscape should complement each other and find the middle ground between nature and human action. This bench had functional lines and adapts to the environment in an unobtrusive way.

0399 The members of East have decided to take a proactive stance in terms of the maintenance of street furniture. To prevent vandalism of these benches and to help educate people, plaques were installed with poems and texts written in workshops held at nearby schools.

0400 According to Ishtmus, one of the best strategies to design any type of street furniture or structure in exterior spaces is to observe and understand the site. Looking at, listening to and feeling the nature of the environment are actions that have a positive impact on the final design.

0401 The resources used by De Amicis Architetti for Piazza Incontro tra i Popoli (covers, tables and chairs, circular benches around the trees, etc.) achieve a functional distribution of space that brings together small areas of grass and a circulation area.

0402 Courtyard furniture next to the Inktpot building in Utrecht, the Netherlands, can be moved and their position and quantity can vary. Okra designers created mobile flower pots and seats that adapt to the space according to the needs of the moment.

0403 The black granite cubes by Landskap Design in Sverres Square serve to guide traffic from one side of the street to the other and to give the space its own personality. The polished side of the cubes faces the traffic so they can reflect the headlights.

0404 While the design of this public space reinterprets the former Hanseatic city, the design of the furniture was created in line with contemporary settings. The seats, designed for a short stay, are, for Okra Landschapsarchitecten, the monuments of the future.

0405 Often, when public spaces undergo a renovation, older equipment is often discarded. In End Street Park, members of Newtown Landscape Architects reused several elements for the paving and combined them with other new elements, such as the benches surrounding the playground.

0406 Mayer Van Heekplein Square had become a parking lot and was only used by locals for the weekly market. Okra and West 8 rearranged and restored this space. Even at night, the square is now illuminated by the benches.

0404

0406

0405

0407 This furniture, designed by Rehwaldt Landschaftsarchitekten and located along the shore of a lake, takes into account the space and environmental impact on the land. The intervention is diluted in a space of large dimensions.

0408 The work by RMP Stephan Lenzen Landschaftsarchitekten is based on plants. In the T Mobile project, the furniture helps to create order and use the wild qualities of the plants.

0409 The Bundesgartenschau project in Koblenz, Germany, by RMP Stephan Lenzen Landschaftsarchitekten, stands out by reinforcing the already present elements and by incorporating new elements such as furniture and lighting.

0410 Playgrounds are not only for children. Rehwaldt Landschaftsarchitekten propose recreational elements for all ages, and it is the design that makes the place special.

0407

0408

0409

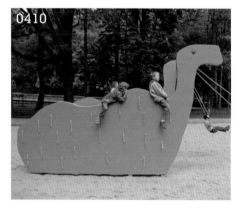

0410

0411

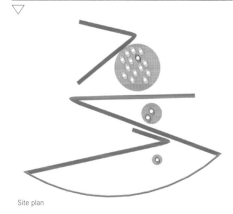

Site plan

0414

0412

0413

0411 Land by Sandra Aguilar proposes that public facilities and spaces are objects in their own right. The Aceituna seats were designed with the aim of becoming a meeting place, where you can rest and watch the world go by, enriching the architecture of the plaza.

0412 The installation of street furniture in Quincy Court has revitalized an underused area among the buildings of Chicago, Illinois, according to Rios Clementi Hale Studios. Also, as it is now a busier area, it creates a greater sense of security among users.

0413 For the design of these benches, Rehwaldt Landschaftsarchitekten have followed these maxims: the design must follow the initial concept from start to finish. For the architects, the plants, materials and colors should match.

0414 Sasaki studio is responsible for the design of the furniture in the Bates Promenade. When design and functionality are integrated they can transform any outdoor space into an elegant space with its own identity.

0415 The blue ends of the benches of the Arts Block University College, Dublin, Ireland, designed by Stephen Diamond Associates, light up at dusk and cheer up the space along with the flowerbed lighting, encouraging more people to make use of the space.

0416 Strootman Landschapsarchitecten designers carried out two renovations in the courtyards of the Eusebiushof Building. In one of the courtyards, trees have been planted in a built-in bench, a change that has given the space personality and a unique character.

0417 Public spaces come to life when they are used. In the Stadtpark Uster, Switzerland, by Schweingruber Zulauf Landschaftsarchitekten, the street furniture is a structure that becomes the point of origin of the activity of the space.

0418 The secondary ideas of a project must not weaken the message. In the Harbour Park in Jonkoping, Sweden, terraces have been ordered so that they are also used as benches, but without losing their function.

0419 The philosophy of design at different scales allows Strootman Landschapsarchitecten to undertake projects of varied sizes. On this occasion, they designed furniture for the River Aa area in Drenthe, the Netherlands.

0420 The members of Taylor Cullity Lethlean consider the details that form the project. The reclinable seats and wooden slats of these benches at the University of Sydney, Australia, are the key elements of a design that people will remember.

0421 For Thomas Balsley Associates, it is important to reflect on the occupation of public spaces. For the Gantry Plaza State Park project in New York, they questioned whether or not the park was really designed for users, and they changed the design of the benches.

0422 Thomas Balsley Associates dared to innovate the street furniture of Maine Street Park in Dallas, Texas. Covered seating areas allow the park to be used more often.

0423

0424

0425

0426

0427

0423 For the National Garden Show, held in Schwerin, Germany, Topotek landscape architects designed a picnic area in a floodplain in order to beat the heat and allow the public to cool off.

0424 The color of the furniture in Chapultepec Park, designed by Mario Schjetnan from GDU, manages to bring out elements that are usually fused with the surroundings.

0425 Thomas Balsley Associates reinterpret public space in all their projects, and in Maine Street Park in Dallas, Texas, they combine conventional architectural elements, such as the deck, with other more natural elements, such as stone benches.

0426 This aesthetic and colorful acrylic seat designed by TN+ Paysagistes Associés creates a visual contrast with the austerity of the buildings surrounding the plaza, which date from the 1970s.

0427 Danse en Ligne is a space between two blocks of buildings. To promote the use of this site and to achieve better communication between neighbors, the architects of NIPpaysage fitted the space with modern and bright pistachio-colored furniture.

0428 These examples of furniture by Turenscape studio in Tianjin Qiaoyuan Park and Qinhuangdao Red Ribbon Park show how to integrate artificial elements in a cluttered landscape, thus bringing some order into the environment.

0428

0429

0430

0431

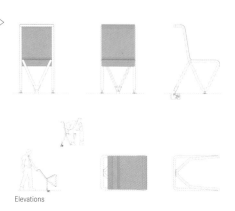

Elevations

0432

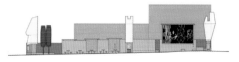

Elevations

0429 Obra Architects designed furniture specifically for the Beatfuse! project. The wooden deck chairs are incorporated into the poolside by a dovetail joint.

0430 Rudolf Bednar Park, by Hager Landschaftsarchitektur, is in the new Leopoldstadt district in Vienna, Austria. The park consists of several areas, including a playground designed so that children of various ages can jump, climb or swing.

0431 In the Largo da Devesa Square in Portugal, designed by the architectural studio Mateo Arquitectura, light and dynamic street furniture has been installed, some of which is movable so it can suit the different needs of the space.

0432 In this passageway, located between two shopping centers, Rios Clementi Hale Studios designed light towers with benches that simulate chess pieces. They also installed 16 tables with various boards and extra seats.

0433 Tejo Remter & René Veenhuizen designed a fence surrounding the Het Noorderlicht School and made use of a few projections and curves to incorporate benches made with the same materials as the fence.

0434 The renovation of the Promenade of Light, designed by Tonkin Liu, has restored an underutilized area for pedestrians. In the trees, circles have been installed that serve several functions. Some of them are benches and ledges offering rest areas for pedestrians.

0435 The Riva waterfront in the city of Split, Croatia, is a design by 3LHD. The paving, consisting of stone slabs, sets the standard for how the other items are positioned: street furniture, flowerbeds, etc.

0436 Stephan Becsei and Christine Hackenbracht are founding architects of B.A.E.R. studio. In their designs for Heinz Raspe Square, they decided to install a long bench, consisting of strips of wood, which marks the border between the natural spaces and the cement floor of the square.

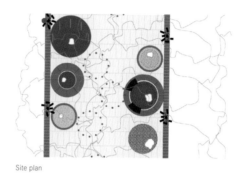

Site plan

0437 The recovery of this important enclave in Sydney, Australia, allowed the city to gain a new public space. The street furniture, which combines wood and concrete, is one of the better-integrated elements in the overall design by ASPECT Studios.

0438 Whether as seats or as elements of protection, the flexibility of the architectural elements of the exterior spaces of the Faculty of Science of the UMD, a project by oslund.and.assoc., gives the space a sculptural character.

0439 In the Gold Medal Park, by oslund.and.assoc., all the architectural elements are sustainable. An LED panel system makes the modules with benches into sources of light at nighttime.

0440

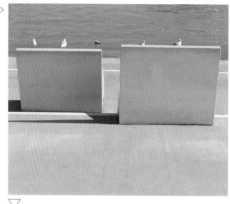

0441

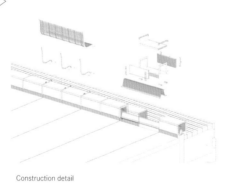

Construction detail

0442

0440 These concrete benches, made by Paolo Bürgi for Lakefront Square, are painted in soft colors to add warmth and break the coldness of the urban space's concrete furniture and gray cement floor.

0441 The benches of Battery Park City Streetscapes New York, by James Carpenter, combine two functions: seating and lighting. The molten glass base creates a solid light volume on which the metal structure rests, forming the seat and backrest.

0442 These wooden benches elegantly surround the tree pits in Piazza Castello, Italy. For this furniture, designer Paolo Bürgi has combined materials such as Douglas fir wood and stainless steel.

0443 Michele & Miquel Architectes & Paysagistes were in charge of renovating the town square of Arles-sur-Tech, France. The space stands out for the uniform gray cement floor. The angles of the street furniture attempt to break the uniformity of the paving.

0444 Jason Carlow, from Carlow Architecture and Design, designed this bamboo and Corian bench for public spaces. The modular system allows the benches to be adapted to every space and surface.

0445 Auböck & Kárász designed a square in the Austrian town of Hall, near Innsbruck, purposed for two activities: going for a walk and relaxing. The walking area surrounds the square, and in the center, the wooden benches provide a comfortable space to relax in a bamboo garden.

0446 TYIN tegnestue members designed houses for refugee children from Noh Bo, Thailand. The project provides an important residential and community space and outdoor furniture where children can play and interact.

0447 Elena Goday and Christoph Tönges from CON-BAM show that sustainability can be applied to any construction. They designed a bamboo bench without glues or screws. The only fixing element is four straps.

0448 The High Line, a former rail line converted into an urban park, incorporates natural materials in mobile outdoor furniture, which counteracts the industrial aesthetic of the structure.

0449

0450

0451

0452

0453

0449 The Urban Lounge by Carlos Martínez and Pipi-lotti Rist is a set of street furniture that impresses with its soft, organic forms and the power of the color red. The furniture completely changes the perception of the public space where it is located.

0450 According to ASPECT Studios, you must strive so that public spaces, whether for temporary or permanent renovations, provide moments of joy and happiness to the users. In the Meeting Place project, the use of the color yellow energizes and enlivens the space.

0451 Stephen Diamond Associates strategically placed the Arts Block benches at University College Dublin, Ireland, to encourage communication and inter-action of students and to facilitate entry to the building.

0452 Stephen Diamond Associates retains, integrates and considers the meaning of the context of an existing landscape. In the IADT campus project, materials such as wood, Corten steel and granite were used to create a meeting and contemplation space with wooden seats and a pond.

0453 For the members of Sasaki, the poetic use of materials (in the case of the Sacred Heart benches, cement, wood and stone) can create landscapes that integrate architecture with nature and provide meeting spaces for use throughout the year.

0454 This haven for cyclists in Grunnfør, Norway, provides rest and a landscape. The design by 70°N Arkitektur allows a discreet presence in the landscape and 360-degree views of the landscape surrounding this small building.

0455 Normal activities of urban life transform this urban plaza into an interactive space. The architects of 1/1 Architecture have designed a space that respects the historic atmosphere from the Selimiye Mosque and fuses it with the existing urban spirit.

0456 For 100 Landschaftsarchitektur, a garden is a space in which to play and experiment. Even an industrial zone can be a garden. This ephemeral port garden includes water (which, ironically, is almost inaccessible in this port) and becomes a tangible and unclassifiable element.

0454

0455

0456

0457

0458

0459

Sketch

0460

0457 In this installation, called Flying Zebras, the architects at 100 Landschaftsarchitektur interpreted the daily traffic as a dance number. The crosswalk is blurred in space and opens the door to reflection on public space and the different users: pedestrians, cyclists, etc.

0458 Repetition is not monotonous, it is dynamic. For the national event Imaginez Maintenant, the architects of Atelier Altern designed an installation in which a common object, such as wooden staves, creates a kinetic effect that transforms the space.

0459 For ASPECT Studios architects, the traditional monuments emphasize the vertical, static and frontal elements of the design. In Memorial to the Emergency Services in Canberra, Australia, a horizontal, dynamic and tactile monument has been created.

0460 Sculptures are an important part of the cityscape. These figures representing soldiers are part of the sculpture dedicated to General Maister, the work of Bruto Landscape Architecture. They stand out for the material, thick wire, and blue lights that light up at dusk.

0461 The Crazy Carpet Project, by Cardinal Hardy, is an installation for International Flora in Montreal, Canada. Large orange cushions were designed for this space so that users could play, relax, chat, jump, etc.

0462 The users of this park came together to voice their concern about the behavior of some dogs, who scared or disturbed children and other visitors. East studio designed stone slabs to remind owners to control their pets.

0463 According to the Cardinal Hardy architects, it is important to be bold in the installation of sculptures and decorative elements in public spaces. In the Lofts Lowney courtyard in Montreal, Canada, the attractive and surprising image of a cherry is a prominent feature.

0464 According to Francis Landscapes studio, when a garden is well designed, it relates to its surrounding elements and gives pleasure to the senses. In addition, original features that initially attract the visitor, such as these fountains, must be created.

0465 For Idealice, there are many steps between the vision of an idea and its realization. In the center of Innsbruck, they installed a kind of Heummandln, a typical Austrian structure on which to dry grass. This installation is a good way to represent regional traditions.

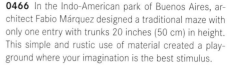

0466 In the Indo-American park of Buenos Aires, architect Fabio Márquez designed a traditional maze with only one entry with trunks 20 inches (50 cm) in height. This simple and rustic use of material created a playground where your imagination is the best stimulus.

0467 Johansson Landskab moved this large Japanese cherry tree, which grew on the site where he was going to build a house, and turned it into a playground for children.

0468 Franklin Children's Garden, a playground in Toronto, Canada, was designed for children. Janet Rosenberg + Associates came up with the idea of showing children the different ecosystems and some of their elements, such as these watering cans, to help them experience nature firsthand.

0469 The LAND-I project for the Insabina Yoga Center involved several renovations. In the garden, Corten steel boxes in which wild plants grow have been installed. This center is surrounded by cultivated fields, making this installation stand out in the landscape.

0470 According to LAND-I, a landscape is never new, it always hides traces of a previous state and is waiting to be discovered and to create a new beginning. The Metropolis project introduces plants in boxes so it looks like they are about to be moved, but the color, smell and shape can still be appreciated.

0471 Lodewijk Baljon Landscape Architects' installation for the Chaumont-sur-Loire Garden Festival reflects on the essence of gardening. A forest of large colored hoes surrounds a space in which a plastic geranium has been surrounded by mirrors.

0472 In the Cornerstone Gardens project in Sonoma, California, LAND-I architects play with scale, the element that traditionally defines and measures space. In this project, they wanted to avoid the predictable and challenge viewers to redefine their reference points.

0473 The Orange Power installation, by LAND-I, brings together 50,000 orange plastic balls in a garden where the color orange predominates. The orange tree was chosen because the tree has been cultivated for 4,000 years and has united the East and West throughout history.

0474 Lodewijk Baljon Landscape Architects created this installation with willows floating in a line on the water for the River Rotte Festival in Rotterdam, the Netherlands, to evoke the source and route of the river outside of the town.

0475 For Land by Sandra Aguilar, it is important to link aesthetics, function and diversity, providing uniqueness to any new space. This project has created playthings with a design inspired by the native species of the place.

0476 For Rankinfraser Landscape Architecture, contrast is important. These giant vertical flowers contrast with the horizontal nature of the vegetation on the terraces. In addition, the nocturnal lighting of these elements transforms the space.

0477 The Espigas de Estancia Grande are sculptures that bring dynamism to the landscape. This design by Land by Sandra Aguilar is based on the agave species and cereals grown in the area.

0478 The designers at Rios Clementi Hale Studios advocate uniting functions and achieving a budget adapted to each project. In the Glendale Chess Park, giant sculptures that light up at night were installed.

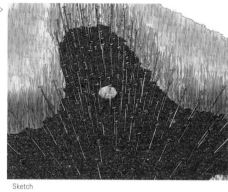

Sketch

Photomontage

0474

0476

0475

0477

0478

0479 One of the maxims of the landscape architects at Strijdom van der Merwe is to work around the existing landscape. They used the sides of the road at the Gilloolys junction of the highway in Johannesburg, South Africa, to welcome visitors to the World Cup 2010.

0480 This installation by Strijdom van der Merwe, entitled Environmental Prayers/Poems Blowing in the Wind, was created with 60 eco-themed haikus written by 60 poets and printed on fabric exhibited in the landscape. The wind turns the messages into visual poems.

0481 This project by Land by Sandra Aguilar seeks to break the linear continuity of the landscape along a highway. This circular plant container made of stones intervenes in the landscape and changes the common perception of the boundaries of these infrastructures.

0482

0483

0484

Photomontage

0482 Unlike with architecture, in landscape design, human measurement is not used as a reference, as the relevant scale is what you see. Thorbjörn Andersson, of Sweco Architects, has installed four large pots in Stenbeck Square with vegetation from around the world.

0483 Here, Strijdom van der Merwe studio wrapped 393 trees on Dorp Street in Stellenbosch, South Africa, in red cloth. The aim was to use natural elements to create a beautiful landscape and simultaneously send out a hidden message.

0484 For the outdoor spaces of Osaka World Trade Center, Japan, Thomas Balsley Associates architects designed a sculptural installation with large cones in a pond. It was intended to become an icon in the landscape.

0485 PLANT Architect were the winners of the competition to design the war veteran park in the Dublin Grounds of Remembrance in Ohio. This structure is one of the elements of a space that is an environment for reflection, contemplation and to honor the union of the community.

0486 Claude Cormier Architectes Paysagistes created the Solange installation for a gardening festival. Artificial flowers reflect nature, and the choice of silk makes reference to the historical importance of the textile industry in Lyon, France.

0487 In the context of a garden fair, Green Shift, a work by NIPpaysage, is a garden and a playground at the same time. The garden is a sculptural embankment wrapped in several green elements of different textures combined with vegetation.

0488 The natural process of decomposition has an artistic component in this case. Werner Henkel, of NaturArte, forms the German word *werden* ("to transform") with six compost bins to convey his message.

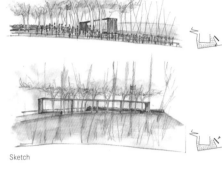

Sketch

Sketch

Photomontage

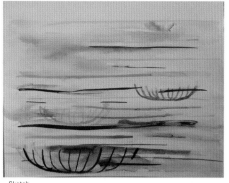

Sketch

0491

Sketch

0492

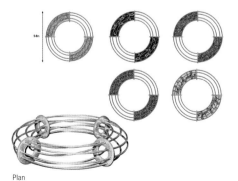

Plan

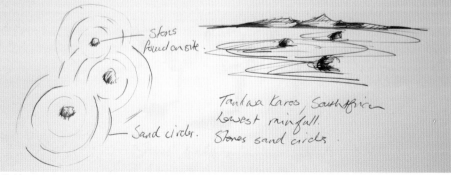

Sketch

0489 Artist Marja Hakala built this dreamboat on the River Jämsä which provided a link across the river and transport for the Between Bridges exhibition. According to the artist, in dreams you can travel anywhere...

0490 Here artist Strijdom van der Merwe has created a circular structure of branches found on the site. This work, entitled Eremo, creates a space for introspection and reflection.

0491 The value of the Zero Waste facility, designed by Oxigen, is based on finding a solution that combines an artistic work with an active plan that is committed to the environment. These structures take into account the currents and the interaction of marsh birds with the environment.

0492 Landscape artist Strijdom van der Merwe likes to work surrounded by nature. Geometry is often present in his creations. The Sand Circles project merges nature and its transience.

0493 Glasser und Dagenbach designed the Moabit Prison Historical Park in Germany which features a concrete cube located in a circular space that was once the main surveillance zone of the former prison.

0494 This pavilion, by David A. García and located in Beijing, China, is an experimental project. The woven bamboo structure is stable and does not require any type of union. It can be used as a facade, roof, column, etc.

0495 This design by McGregor Coxall for Ballast Point Park in Sydney, Australia, incorporates many elements that improve its environmental sustainability. The turbines, in addition to providing energy, are one of the sculptural objects of the park and an educational element.

0496 This temporary project, a work by nArchitects, was built in the MoMA courtyard in New York City, New York, as part of a festival for young architects. Bamboo is used as a representation of a wooded landscape.

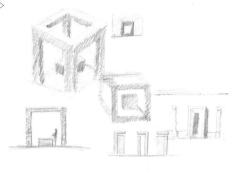

Sketches

Sketch

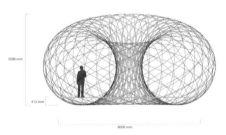

Elevation

0497

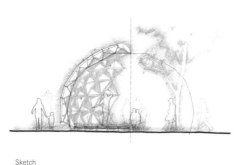

Sketch

0498

0499

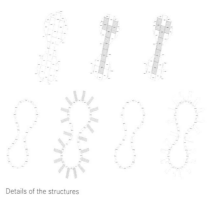

Details of the structures

0500

Sketch

0497 Boo Tech is a prototype designed by Studio Cárdenas members consisting of a geodesic dome built of bamboo and tissue. This sculptural structure, located in the Italian city of Milan, showcases the architectural properties of bamboo.

0498 Bug Dome is the name of the Casagrande Laboratory Taiwan project. It is constructed with bamboo and was inspired by the morphology of insects and built with traditional craftsmanship. It symbolizes a safe haven for the modern person who wants to escape the contemporary urbanism in the city of Shenzhen, China.

0499 The Beatfuse! project consisted of shell-shaped structures covering a triangular space. The spaces defined by these temporary structures, works by Obra Architects, were filled with themes to enjoy the outdoors: a caldarium, an area with sand and barbecues, etc.

0500 Terragram studio, now Room 4.1.3, carried out several renovations at the Garden of Australian Dreams and the National Museum of Australia. One of them is this sculpture: a path that seems to lift off the ground and rise above the surface.

0501

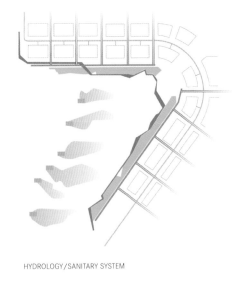

HYDROLOGY/SANITARY SYSTEM

BACTERIA BREAK-DOWN CHAMBER
Settling, anaerobic digestion, separation of blackwater and sludge
BIOFILTRATION CELLS
Step-by-step cleansing of blackwater via vegetation
WEIR
Storage of treated water for re-use
HILLTOP BIOSOLID RE-USE
Drying, release of compost to soil for vegetal growth

Master plan of Parque Aguasverde in Madrid, Spain by Landworks Studio

0502

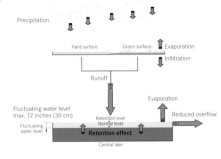

Stormwater management diagram for Fornebu Park designed by Björbek Lindheim in collaboration with Atelier Dreiseitl

0503

0504

0505

0506

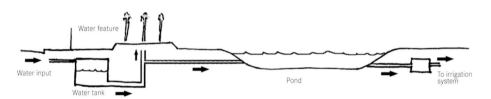

Scheme of water use for the Flora Nativa Benito Quinquela Martín by Fabio Márquez

Water feature

Water input

Water tank

Pond

To irrigation system

0507

Section renderings of the Berkel-Pijnacker green zone

0508

Partial master plan of the Isar River management work

Plan of the Berkel-Pijnacker green zone by H+N+S
Landschapsarchitecten

0501 The site responds to the realities of water limitations by maximizing efficiency of storm-water and exploiting wastewater as a potential new supply. This infrastructural landscape yields a dynamic set of spaces, addresses recreational and social needs, and stimulates economic and ecological growth.

0502 An artificial lake is a critical feature of Fornebu Park in Oslo, Norway. It is a storm-water basin accommodating precipitation that is dependent on fluctuating water levels. Overflow water feeds the "frogland" — a wetland that serves as habitat to various species — before slowly seeping into the Oslo Fjord.

0503 The park constitutes a storm water system that collects rainwater and spring snowmelt. The water is cleaned and slowly released to a wetland via swales whose soft topography mirrors the flow of water.

0504 Michael Singer collaborated with Behnisch and Partner and Copijn Tuin en Landschaps Architecten on the Alterra Institute for Environmental Research in Wageningen, the Netherlands. The gardens function as the "lungs and kidneys" of the building, cleaning air and gray water, as well as providing comfortable climate control.

0505 Flora Nativa Benito Quinquela Martín Park in Buenos Aires, Argentina, benefits from a water recycling system that was implemented to avoid wasting water. Water flows first through a water jet play area before it falls in a pond that supplies the irrigation system, which is composed of sprinklers and drip hoses.

0506 Water, including potential runoff and storm water, needs to be dealt with responsibly. Simple yet innovative design decisions can reduce a landscape's water requirements, reduce runoff and increase water quality.

0507 The transformation of a large polder in the Randstad Holland, the Netherlands, area composed of large-scale built-up areas, needed a robust green-blue counterbalance. As a response, a ribbon of parks fulfills recreational needs and provides water storage.

0508 The design scheme for the banks of the Isar River in downtown Munich, Germany, applies built elements only where they are inevitable for flood protection, giving center stage to the fast-flowing river with its gravel banks and meadows.

0509 At the Oregon Convention Center in Portland, Mayer/Reed demonstrated with The Rain Garden how vegetated green infrastructure cleans and treats storm water within a narrow $1/2$-acre (2,000 m^2) site.

0510 A development scheme on the Bronx side of Highbridge, New York, would provide a gateway to the aqueduct. Configured as a loop, it intertwines street and bridge accesses and continues as a pathway that leads down to the existing river access.

0511 PEG office of landscape + architecture created a system that incorporates art, recreation and landscape and utilizes the steel and masonry structure of a bridge. A series of infra-blooms collect and filter rainfall, then channel it back to the bridge, where it falls, days later, into the Harlem River.

0512 The hillside of a residential complex by the sea was transformed into a plant-filled terraced courtyard in response to the need for drainage. The project was developed around a water theme and takes advantage of existing elements on the site.

0513 Viet Village Urban Farm is a flat site lacking positive drainage. To facilitate irrigation of the crops, multiple access points for water are provided. The runoff from irrigation is drained back to the central location through a series of bio-swales to aid water cleansing.

0510

Infra-blooms plan

Computer-generated rendering by PEG office of landscape + architecture

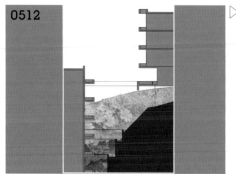

Section diagram through courtyard designed by R&R Rencoret y Ruttimann Arquitectura y Paisaje

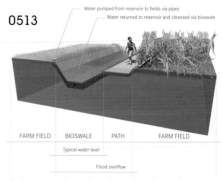

Section diagram through farm site developed by Spackman, Mossop + Michaels

0514

0515

0516

0517

0518

0514 In Shanghai Houtan Park, China, designed by Turenscape, the banded pattern of the plants dramatizes the filtrating and cleaning function of the wetland.

0515 Tianjin Qiaoyuan Park, China, by Turenscape, has simple dug out ponds to catch storm water and lets nature do the rest of the work.

0516 Drip irrigation makes optimal use of both water and fertilizer. It allows for irrigation of irregularly shaped fields and permits water to infiltrate directly to the roots of the plants through a system of pipes and drippers.

0517 Gardena offers an automatic system that can water up to 36 potted plants. Irrigation is activated daily using a transformer with a timer. There are three water flows according to the needs of each plant.

0518 Drip irrigation or localized irrigation uses up to 60% less water compared to traditional irrigation systems, and fertilizer loss is minimized thanks to localized application and reduced leaching.

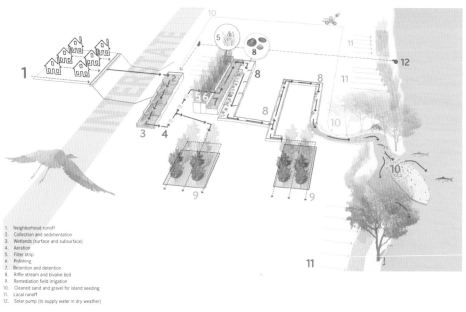

1. Neighborhood runoff
2. Collection and sedimentation
3. Wetlands (surface and subsurface)
4. Aeration
5. Filter strip
6. Polishing
7. Retention and detention
8. Riffle stream and bivalve bed
9. Remediation field irrigation
10. Cleaned sand and gravel for island seeding
11. Local runoff
12. Solar pump (to supply water in dry weather)

Storm water runoff management diagram

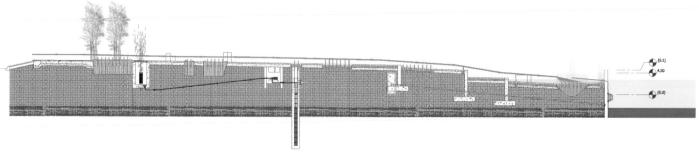

Section diagram of water management

0524

0525

0519 Sprinklers can reach as far as 20 feet (6 m) depending on the pressure and nozzle used. The different directions of programmable sprinklers reach every corner and adapt to any landscape configuration.

0520 A water-cleansing system structures a park. Wetlands of nutrient-tolerant species receive the storm water, removing sediment and pollutants. Meanwhile, local runoff in the park flows through filter strips and into polishing wetlands connected to the system.

0521 This illustration shows a Graf rainwater collection tank that allows users to water their yard. A green roof can retain between 50% and 90% of rainwater, while the rest can be collected for future use.

0522 The green roof of the Academy of Sciences building in San Francisco, California, designed by Renzo Piano, is planted with species that do not require artificial irrigation. The roof retains as much as 70% of the rainwater, preventing it from becoming runoff.

0523 Erie Street Plaza by Stoss Landscape Urbanism activates and registers environmental cycles of storm water by collecting runoff to support a reconstituted marsh/wetland. It re-charges the groundwater and utilizes river water for irrigation.

0524 To resolve the irrigation of this vertical garden composed of 12,000 hydroponic ferns, R&Sie(n) used an individual mechanical drop-by-drop system that feeds on rainwater collected in 300 glass beakers mounted on a flexible steel structure.

0525 Drainage backups, root puncture or the inappropriate selection of waterproofing membrane system, root barrier and/or drainage layer can cause a roof to leak. Also, an excess of water in the soil will adversely affect the plants, which will drown or rot.

0526

Scheme for the campus and park of the Infineon headquarter in Munich, Germany, by GTL Gnüchtel Triebswetter Landschaftsarchitekten

0527

0528

0. Pre treatment
1. Reed filters
2. Infiltration in sand
3. Reed and iris filters in the last pond

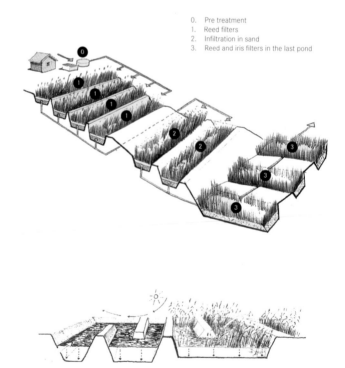

Diagram of water treatment for Los Itzicuaros Park in Mexico by GDU

0526 A natural lake of 20 acres (8 ha) surrounds the campus of the Infineon headquarters in Munich, Germany. Apart from its aesthetic qualities, the lake works as a climatic buffer to reduce peak temperatures. A large-scale reed and sand filtration system keeps the water at top quality.

0527 This project for a new public park on the heavily contaminated site of a former gas factory presented a problem that could only be resolved with an ecological point of view. The remaining basement structure of the gasholders has been transformed into a contemplative water-lily pool and verdant aquatic garden.

0528 The topographical and hydrologic conditions and the contact with an existing drainage channel present the opportunity to create a unique lacustrian park that contributes to the biological treatment of black-water. The bodies of water are designed to activate the biological treatment, to attract migratory birds and to provide opportunities for recreational activities.

0529

0529 CMG is responsible for the design of a 16-acre (6 ha) regional storm water treatment wetland and trail system. The design, which combines infrastructure and water quality functions, responds to hydraulic requirements, water quality parameters, public access, maintenance considerations and the creation of habitats.

0530 A former shooting range used as a garbage dump was transformed into a low-maintenance urban park through storm water containment and purification, the improvement of the saline-alkali soil and the recuperation of the native landscape. This provided opportunities for environmental education and the creation of a sustainable landscape.

0531 The ChonGae Sunken Stone Garden is part of the redevelopment effort by the city of Seoul to restore a highly polluted and covered canal. The demolition of nearly 4 miles (6.4 km) of at-grade and elevated highway infrastructure that divided the city led to the creation of a green corridor that brings people closer to the historic ChonGae Canal.

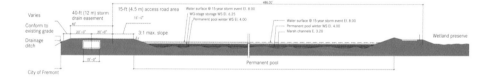

Site sections

0530

0531

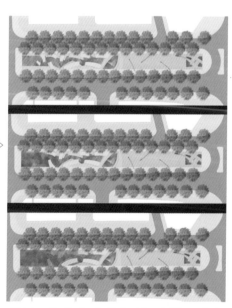

Tidal plans of the ChonGae Canal in Seoul, Korea, by Mikyoung Kim in collaboration with SeoAhn Total Landscape

0532 The Australian office of landscape architects Oxigen designed Thorndon Park in Adelaide as a new recreational park. It occupies the grounds of a former industrial infrastructure and introduces new forms and spaces, such as wetlands that recirculate the water from a reservoir and purify incoming storm water from nearby residential suburbs.

0533 Leidsche Rijn Park, designed by West 8, is a green zone in a recently built residential neighborhood of Utrecht, the Netherlands. It is delimited by three edges formed by a re-excavated meander of the Rhine River. The result is a long ecological zone with rich flora that attracts a wide variety of animals.

0534 C. F. Møller created a man-made lake area derived from the need to excavate gravel. In some areas, the excavation reached a depth of 23 feet (7 m), resulting in deep groundwater, while less deep lakes generated shallow habitats for rare amphibians.

0535

0536

Stork Project scheme by H+N+S Landschapsarchitecten

0537

0535 Viet Village Urban Farm is an urban farming project in eastern New Orleans, Louisiana, an area hard hit by Hurricane Katrina. Spackman, Mossop + Michaels assisted the community with the design of environmental infrastructural systems that were needed to support an organic urban farming operation.

0536 The natural dynamic process of the big Dutch rivers with seasonal flooding is used to transform the river floodplains from agricultural land to wet nature areas. The widening of the river is combined with the development of new natural values, with the black stork as an icon.

0537 Within a very sensitive environment of pine forest, steep ravines, and hydrologic systems, SWA restored balance through reforestation and watershed planning. Contiguous areas of open space were preserved while new development focused on preexisting disturbed areas.

0538 To mark the entrance to the city of Östersund in Sweden, Gora Art & Landscape placed six blue reinforced fiberglass sculptures at an important traffic junction. During the day, the sculptures, which are about the size of a car, make a big impression; at night, the sculptures emit a turquoise light, providing the site with a distinct identity.

0539 Lighting in landscaped areas should come from a low-level diffusing fixture preferably hidden between bushes or shrubs. This will reduce the glare from the exposed source when looking at the landscape from a far angle.

0540 Wrapped in perforated stainless steel and dichroic resin panels, the barcode patterns of the lanterns placed in front of the Ocean County Public Library in Toms River, New Jersey, represent the transmission of data and digital information networks.

0541 Gora Art & Landscape designed a series of 11 1/2-foot (3.5 m) tall cones made of expanded wire mesh placed in a large expanse of flat land in Tierp, Sweden. During the day, the metallic cones shimmer with sunlight; at night the cones are illuminated from within, changing color very slowly as one drives past them.

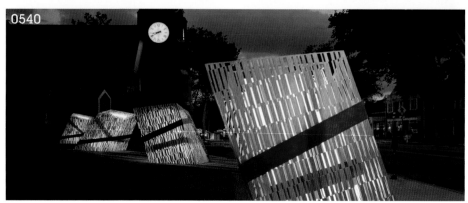

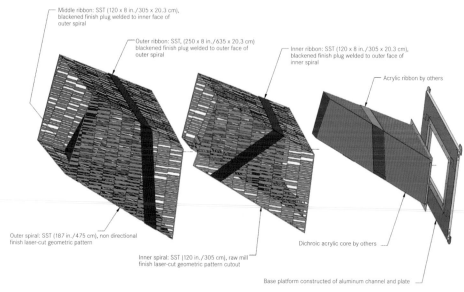

Middle ribbon: SST (120 x 8 in./305 x 20.3 cm), blackened finish plug welded to inner face of outer spiral

Outer ribbon: SST, (250 x 8 in./635 x 20.3 cm) blackened finish plug welded to outer face of outer spiral

Inner ribbon: SST (120 x 8 in./305 x 20.3 cm), blackened finish plug welded to outer face of inner spiral

Acrylic ribbon by others

Outer spiral: SST (187 in./475 cm), non directional finish laser-cut geometric pattern

Inner spiral: SST (120 in./305 cm), raw mill finish laser-cut geometric pattern cutout

Dichroic acrylic core by others

Base platform constructed of aluminum channel and plate

Diagram of the lanterns' different parts

0542

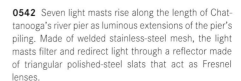

0542 Seven light masts rise along the length of Chattanooga's river pier as luminous extensions of the pier's piling. Made of welded stainless-steel mesh, the light masts filter and redirect light through a reflector made of triangular polished-steel slats that act as Fresnel lenses.

0543 Molard Square in Geneva, Switzerland, occupies the space of a lake port that existed in the Middle Ages. The repaving design of the square, by 2b Architectes, integrates resin blocks that are lit at night. The concept is a metaphor for the lake. To reinforce the visual effect, words have been chiseled into the resin blocks.

0544 La Familia, by Gora Art & Landscape, is based on the idea of creating a garden experience in the infection clinic of Malmö, Sweden. Due to strict restrictions in this sensitive environment, plants could not be used. Instead, the garden experience was achieved through polyester reinforced fiber-glass sculptures.

0545 Find your own sources of inspiration. Look, travel, discuss. Inspiration for the Jimmy Project came from the Kata Tjuta (Olga) rock formation near Uluru (Ayers Rock), in Australia.

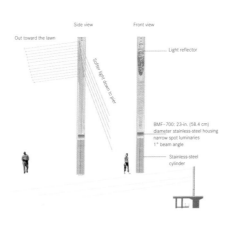

Side view Front view

Out toward the lawn

Softer light down to pier

Light reflector

BMF–700: 23-in. (58.4 cm) diameter stainless-steel housing narrow spot luminaries 1° beam angle

Stainless-steel cylinder

Side and front view of the light masts designed by James Carpenter

0543

MERCI

0545

0544

0546

0547

0548

0549

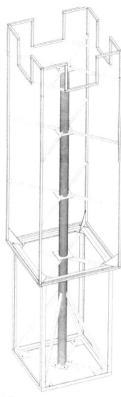

Rook working drawing

0546 While the design of the public realm reinterprets the ancient city, urban furniture is designed as contemporary items. Regarding artificial light, Okra opted for indirect lighting, which provides a fairytale-like effect and a more even spreading of the light.

0547 In order to address the difficulties of growing plants on a balcony where soil cannot be used, N-tree used non-living low-maintenance materials, borrowing from nature. Cube lights placed among white pebbles supply the fantasy of a night scene and harmonize with the surrounding space.

0548 Dutch landscape architects Okra designed a grid of light poles and recessed lighting in the pavement of the station area of Enschede. Part of a larger urban development, this image shows a view of one of three squares that are devoted to the idea of transferring from railway to another transport system.

0549 At the Chess Park in Glendale, California, rather than go through several trades, Rios Clementi Hale Studios worked with an art fabricator to create giant synthetic canvas lantern sculptures that were craned into place.

0550 Use renewable energy if possible, especially to create original light beacons. This very odd and unimproved railway site under regeneration in Paris, France, has been transformed by Roger Narboni, of Concepto studio, into an important urban park that is easily identified at night by its blue beacons.

0551 Garscube Landscape Link is an underpass that connects the cultural quarter of Glasgow, Scotland, with the city center. Rankinfraser Landscape Architecture transformed an unpleasant environment into a vibrant space composed of a series of aluminum flowers that evoke a memory of a park that once occupied the site.

0550

0551

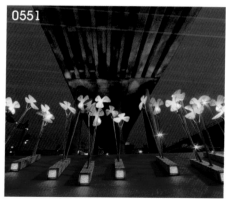

0552 A composition made of playful objects is inspired by the native species of the mountainous landscape. The design links aesthetics, function and diversity, while bringing uniqueness to a new recreational space created by artist Sandra Aguilar.

0553 Try to find a sensitive approach for simple lighting projects. Roger Narboni, of Concepto studio, provides a common pedestrian path through a suburban tree-planted area near Paris, France, with identity and originality.

0554 In the redevelopment of the village center of Keldonk in the Netherlands, Strootman Landschapsarchitecten adapted an off-the-shelf lamp to a site-specific design to create an atmospheric illumination scheme that helps define the character of the village.

0555 Light should be integral to the design of landscape concepts, not an afterthought. Thomas Balsley Associates used rows of light wands as visual markers that imply direction for the Kasumigaseki Plaza renewal.

0556 At the Royal Dublin Society, Ireland, Stephen Diamond Associates applies an abstracted interpretation of woodland, fields, plough lines and fieldstone walls for the design of a new public square, revealing the institution's connection to agriculture, the arts and the historic use of the site.

0557 The TXL lamp is designed by the Spanish lighting company Marset for outdoor use. Similar to its indoor-use version, TXL stands on a slate base with a shade made of fiberglass.

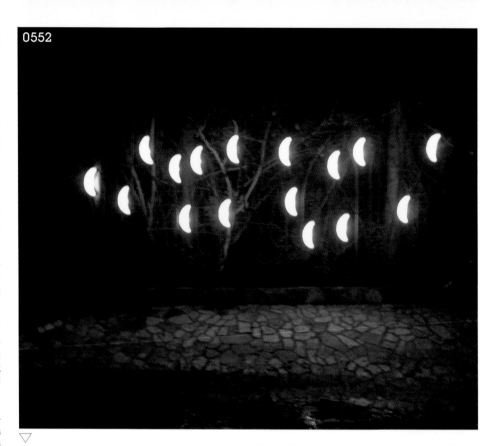

Elevation of the light fixture composition

0555

0556

0557

0558 In addition to brightening up a public space and shedding a spotlight on a part of the landscape that deserves to be showcased, outdoor lighting adds an extra level of security, casting light on pathways to ensure safe footing.

0559 Outdoor living has become an extension of our interior spaces, and lighting design has evolved to enhance the alfresco evening experience. No longer limited to lanterns, beacons and other traditional means to illuminate exterior spaces, new fixtures are innovative, sculptural and energy efficient.

0560 Suitable for cold and hot climates, polycarbonate shells for outdoor lighting stand up to all kinds of weather. These lights animate public spaces, bringing a minimal and sculptural character, which is a nice addition to the patio, garden or terrace of a modern home.

0561 Bloom is a planter that doubles as a light. Made of recyclable polyethylene, it comes in different colors and can be connected to watering and sprinkler systems through a port in its bottom. This port is also the drain for the flowerpot, which enables water to bypass the electrical wiring.

0558

0559

0560

0561

0562

0562 The indefinite character of Erie Street Plaza in Milwaukee, Wisconsin, by Stoss Landscape Urbanism, is accentuated by the erratic scattering of luminous fiberglass benches, which capture and reflect ambient light and project light from within. Their irregular placement allows for multiple and diverse social groupings or solitary retreats.

0563 The Área beacon is a design by Claudi Aguiló and Xavier Nogués for Santa & Cole. Shaped like a tetrahedron and made of a $1/4$-inch (6 mm) thick Corten steel sheet with an inclined stainless-steel reflector, it integrates well into the landscape of the García Sanabria Park in Santa Cruz de Tenerife, Spain, and was remodeled by Palerm & Tabares de Nava Arquitectos.

0563

0564 3.000K Thorn contrast floodlights illuminate water jets emerging from the pavement, adding drama and visual impact. This project by Agence Jacqueline Osty and lighting designer Roger Narboni is part of a large remodel of the city center in Chartres, France.

0565 In one of the remodeled squares of Chartres, a 59-foot (18 m) Aubrilam Eagle Totem lamppost uses the warmth and nobility of the wood to transform this significant structure into a functional sculpture of light.

0566 Stoss Landscape Urbanism's CityDeck in Green Bay, Wisconsin, starts as a simple boardwalk deployed at the edge of city and river. The highly articulated wooden boardwalk undulates, folding in response to programmatic and technical issues, including lighting.

0567 In the remodeling of the boulevards in Chartres, the use of lamps with excellent color rendering created a warm atmosphere at night, redefining the hue of the trees' foliage along the boulevards as well as the tones of the pavement and buildings.

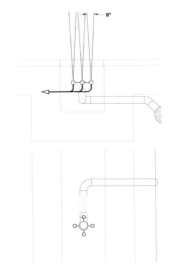

Section and plan of light fixture and water jet under pavement

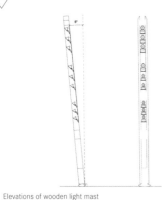

Elevations of wooden light mast

0567

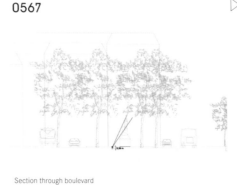

Section through boulevard

0568

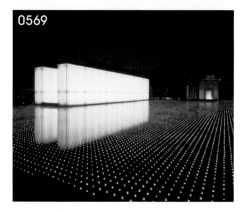

0569

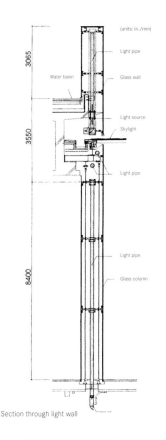

(units: in./mm)

Light pipe

Water basin

Glass wall

Light source

Skylight

Light pipe

Light pipe

Glass column

Section through light wall

0568 At street level, the National Peace Memorial Hall for the Atomic Bomb Victims by Akira Kuryu Architects consists of two parallel light walls that seem to emerge from the black granite pond.

0569 Submerged in the black granite water basin are 70,000 light fibers representing the number of people who died from the Nagasaki bomb's effect. The light fiber tips peer out from tiny holes made in the stone at $3^1/_2$-inch (87 mm) intervals.

0570 The custom bollards created for the Battery Bosque in New York incorporate a bowl that collects rain water. The water catches the light and subtly reflects it up into the trees. The bollards were designed by the lighting company Louis Poulsen and are equipped with Philips 70-watt metal halide lamps.

0571 The paths in Battery Bosque in New York City that lead to the historic harbor are lit with induction post-top lanterns that illuminate low plantings and give dimension to trees. The mix of pole-mounted fixtures and bollards provides enough light to confer a sense of safety.

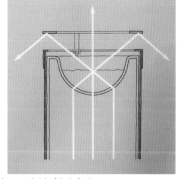

0570

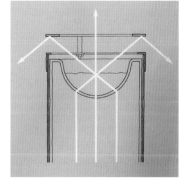

Development sketch of the bollard

Section of the bollard with the water collecting bowl and light refraction effect

0571

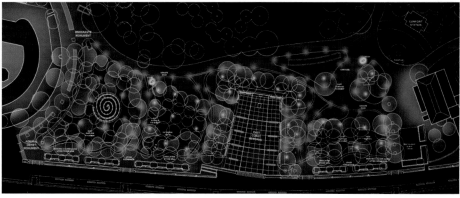

Lighting Fixtures   167

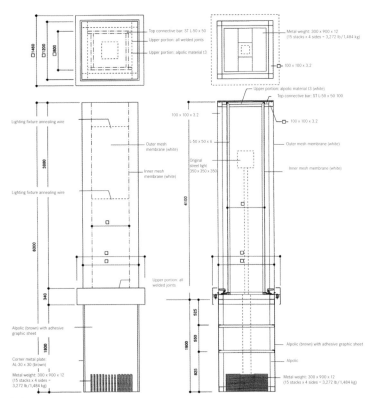

Top connective bar: ST L-50 x 50
Upper portion: all welded joints
Upper portion: alpolic material t3

□1460
□1200
□900

Metal weight: 300 x 900 x 12
(15 stacks x 4 sides = 3,272 lb/1,484 kg)

100 x 100 x 3.2

Upper portion: alpolic material t3 (white)
Top connective bar: ST L-50 x 50 100

100 x 100 x 3.2
100 x 100 x 3.2

Lighting fixture annealing wire

3880

Outer mesh membrane (white)
L-50 x 50 x 6

Outer mesh membrane (white)

6000

Inner mesh membrane (white)
Original street light 350 x 350 x 350

Inner mesh membrane (white)

Lighting fixture annealing wire

4100

340
525
560
1900
825

Upper portion: all welded joints

Alpolic (brown) with adhesive graphic sheet

1800

Alpolic (brown) with adhesive graphic sheet
Alpolic

Corner metal plate: AL-30 x 30 (brown)

Metal weight: 300 x 900 x 12
(15 stacks x 4 sides = 3,272 lb/1,484 kg)

Metal weight: 300 x 900 x 12
(15 stacks x 4 sides = 3,272 lb/1,484 kg)

Construction detail of the lantern

0574

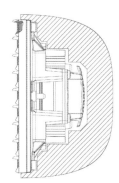

Section through light column

0575

3-D computer model of the ETFE umbrella

0576

0577

0572 This Christmas decoration was inspired by a traditional Japanese element. Along the $^1/_2$-mile (1 km) long road, 60 Japanese-motif lanterns stand 20 feet (6 m) tall and 4 feet (1.2 m) wide. Strings of 1,100 brilliant LEDs and four LED spotlights with 16.7 million color possibilities used in the fixtures were computer controlled.

0573 United Visual Artists collaborated with One-pointsix to produce a light and music installation in the Madejski Garden in front of the Victoria and Albert Museum in London, England. Forty-six columns of LED lights, each equipped with a speaker, are set up in a grid. Light and sound patterns are created by people moving within the grid.

0574 The installation plays with the movement of people walking among the light and sound columns. When moving, every person triggers a brilliant display of light and sound that is different from that set off by others.

0575 Here the Singapore River is making reference to the Chinese lanterns. The umbrellas, made of translucent polytetrafluoroethylene (ETFE), are emphasized with color lighting and provide shading and cooling over the commercial streets of the area.

0576 The guardrails for this footbridge in Coimbra, Portugal, designed by Cecil Balmond and António Adão da Fonseca, incorporate colored glass panes that light up at night to create a suggestive play of light and color over the Mondego River.

0577 Along with an attractive paving and planting scheme, lighting was crucial for EDAW's revitalization of the Haihe River embankment in Tianjin, China, where the poorly fitted lights were replaced with state-of-the-art, energy-efficient fixtures.

0578 SLA has provided the center of Frederiksberg in Denmark with a series of open spaces where change, surprise and heightened awareness of transition are produced through creative light effects.

0579 The stepped concrete water channel that connects the pools in the courtyard of the IBM headquarters in Amsterdam, the Netherlands, creates a stunning effect thanks to the built-in lights that allow people to see the water flow at night.

0580 HtO is an urban beach along the waterfront in Toronto, Canada, designed by Janet Rosemberg + Associates, Claude Cormier Architectes Paysagistes and Hariri Pontarini Architects. At night, the park does not lose any of its attractiveness thanks to the tall light masts that cast soft light on the knolls. Lighting is also programmed to reflect seasons and holidays.

0581 Lighting under a platform elevated from the ground reinforces the ephemeral character of this temporary structure. It also fulfills a safety function in low-light night conditions and offers an alternative to lampposts that may not have been appropriate in this historic architectural context in the center of Innichen in the South Tyrol region of Italy.

Lighting plan for the open spaces of Frederiksberg city center

0582

0582 Ligh-sensitive fluorescent lights housed in the concrete wall create a safe, usable space while also being an attractor at night. This sweeping light effect frames a wetland in Sydney Park, Australia, as part of a recuperation plan of the area carried out by ASPECT Studio.

0583 Molard Square in Geneva, Switzerland, is a cobblestone open area. The surface is punctuated by small translucent resin blocks of the size of the cobbles with embedded LED lights that enliven the square in the evening. Inspired by the sparkling surface of Lake Geneva, the design reinforces the connection between the city and the lake.

0584 As part of a new development near a man-made wetland in Taizhou City, China, designed by Turenscape, a square is built above the flood level so as not to obstruct the seasonal rise of the water level. A floating effect is achieved by the use of glass tiles lit from underneath that allow parts of the ground to be seen from below the square.

0585 This combination of lamppost and water feature is part of the urban renovation of the district of Barleben, Germany. A hanging steel mesh guides a sheet of water down to a pool. The effect is reinforced by the lights in the stainless-steel masts and by the recessed lights at the bottom of the shallow pools.

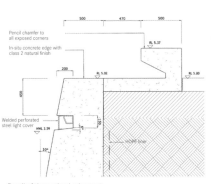

Detail of the wetland-edge seat

0583

0584

0585

Nighttime impression of Barleben's new streetscape designed by Atelier Dreiseitl

0586

0587

0588

0589

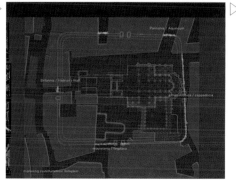

Lighting diagram around Utrecht's Castellum

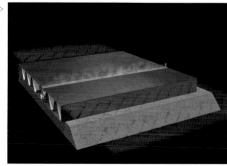

3-D model view of the metal grate set in the pavement designed by
Okra Landschapsarchitecten

0590

0591

0586 For the new Craigiburn Bypass road in Melbourne, Australia, Taylor Cullity Lethlean designed a long acoustic barrier wall of screen-printed acrylic panels with a matrix of color changing LEDs. Every LED fitting is individually controlled and regulated by transducers in the road.

0587 A constellation of lights is set into the timber boards that line the walk that leads to the Darlington Campus of the University of Sydney, Austrlia. Taylor Cullity Lethlean, responsible for the campus's masterplan, achieved this constellation effect by means of holes cut into the wood that were filled with clear resin and lit from underneath.

0588 The urban role of the Meelan, a tributary of the Dijle River, is recuperated as part of a plan to reestablish the historic connection of the old city of Mechelen, Belgium, with water. This project carried out by Okra Landscape Architects includes five bridges that introduce a contrasting contemporary character reinforced by subtle light effects.

0589 A beam of light inset into the pavement around Utrecht's Castellum reinforces the significance of the origin of the Dutch city. The light is especially visible in rainy and misty days or thanks to clouds of smoke that emerge through metal grates.

0590 TROP designed the rooftop of a luxury condominium in a prime Bangkok, Thailand, location. Among other tall buildings, the rooftop is equipped with an L-shaped pool and a garden and benefits from the best views of the city. To preserve some degree of privacy, the rooftop is dimly lit, taking advantage of the light produced by the city skyline.

0591 The Red Ribbon was designed to link and organize the different zones of the Tanghe River Park in Qinhuangdao, China. It winds among a densely vegetated site and integrates seating, environmental interpretation and lighting. Made of red fiber steel, it is lit from inside to glow after dark.

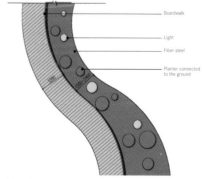

Boardwalk

Light

Fiber steel

Planter connected to the ground

Partial detail of the plan of the Red Ribbon

0592 In response to the fluctuation of tourism that the old town of Innichen, Italy, experiences, the architectural team of AllesWirdGut Architektur has designed a series of temporary installations that can easily be removed after the high season. The designs also include creative lighting effects that reinforce the ephemeral character of the installations.

0593 Specially designed patterns and fiber light points recessed into a concrete surface create a dramatic visual experience. Gobo projectors are mounted on wooden poles to further support the overall maritime design theme conceived by Brandt Landskab for the waterfront promenade in Helsingborg, Sweden

0594 Combining aesthetics and functionality, AllesWirdGut Architektur made an appropriate use of lighting in a public space with steps in the center of Innichen, Italy. In this case, the position of lights was given special consideration to avoid dazzle and glare while creating an attractive visual effect.

0595

0595 The LED and fiber optic technology produce dazzling effects at the Wellness Orhidelia. In the context of this prestigious spa in Slovenia, the soft and diffused light generates a soothing atmosphere while accentuating the innovative architecture created by Enota.

0596 Bruto Landscape Architecture conceived a series of abstract wire frame sculptures for General Maister Memorial Park. Because of the blue light, the composition acts as an illusion at night.

0597 There may be a wish to set up theatrical lighting for special events. On the basis of an overall concept for the revitalization of Aalborg's waterfront by C. F. Møller, a comprehensive lighting plan was developed to equip this area of the Danish city with lighting that enhances the main landscape concept and the city's interface with the harbor.

0596

0597

0598

0599

0600

0598 Never underestimate the importance lighting has in your yards. Yards and gardens are revived at night. Water features and pool lighting techniques are best depicted when one uses multiple small sources rather than a few big flood lights. Lights should be pointed away from the viewer's position in the seating area.

0599 Light and its many forms and effects can be spectacular. A space that is quiet and contemplative by day can be transformed into a stage for celebrations, as is the case at the Old Market Square in Nottingham, England, a project by Gustafson Porter.

0600 A key feature of the North Bayfront Park in Corpus Christi, Texas, is an interactive fountain that attracts children and adults alike. As attractive as fountain may be during the day, it becomes immeasurably more beautiful at night with colorful lights playing upon it.

0601

0601 The Chinese wash painting style for the Hangzhou Grand Canal nightscape in South China was for Roger Narboni, of Concepto studio, a very interesting joint venture done in collaboration with a Chinese lighting group.

0602 This 869-foot (265 m) luminous strip was installed in the riverbed of the Garonne River in Toulouse, France, as part of a lighting master plan for the city. The light fixture is an 8-inch (20 cm) wide and 32-inch (81 cm) long polycarbonate cylinder treated with a transparent resin for waterproofing and strength. Internally, it is fitted with a translucent emitting bar and aluminum reflector lit at each end by one high-intensity blue 1-watt LED.

0603 Paris Front de Seine by Roger Narboni is proof that even in a tough and dense environment one has to think about what urban light can bring to the neighbors in their daily travels.

0604 Rather than lighting up the solid part of an architectural element, emphasizing the openings is an alternative worth considering. Roger Narboni chose to illuminate the Roman Arcueil-Cachan aqueduct near Paris in such a way, turning it into an easily recognizable landmark at night.

0602

0603

0604

0605 The water feature in the courtyard of this residential development designed by Scape Design Associates is an example of how water can be used as a diffuser or conductor of light and color. With light across a spray of water and the glow of water lit from below the surface line, the light dances with the movement of the water.

0606 A unique synergy between architecture, interior design and landscape can be achieved with the use of light to blur boundaries and lead occupants from one space to the next.

0607 Scape Design Associates created a romantic setting for the Knightsbridge, an exclusive residential complex in London, England, with the use of dynamic lighting and a seductive use of fire. In particular, a constellation lighting effect is displayed using fiber optics across the base of a feature lagoon.

0608 Stephen Diamond Associates used energy-saving LEDS to animate the Arts Block Entrance at the University College Dublin, Ireland. Bench ends of blue acrylic signal a new approach to campus, while a halo of green and yellow up-lighters complete the university colors.

0609 Suzhou, China, residents have their own Times Square. SWA used colorful and dynamic lighting effects as the unifying tool to bring eight separate buildings together and create a sense of place that combines the traditional Suzhou culture and a contemporary design language.

0610 Up-lights set in pavement help create a magical atmosphere at nighttime. Birk Nielsen of Sweco combined this effect with a stepped water feature.

0608

0609

0610

0611 Terragram conceived Theater of Lights, a private garden in Sydney, Australia, where fog, fiber optics, the sound of water and traditional lighting are combined to create numerous scenarios during the day and night.

0612 Agence Jacqueline Osty and Roger Narboni conceived a large glass screen as a public art piece representing a lunar landscape. They used 102 Color Kinetics ColorBlast 12 luminaries with LED fittings to create the lighting effect.

0613 A lighting strip can create the perfect edge for your planter box or path. Thanks to its flexibility, this product can be used for wrapping trees and can also be mounted on structures such as edges and coves.

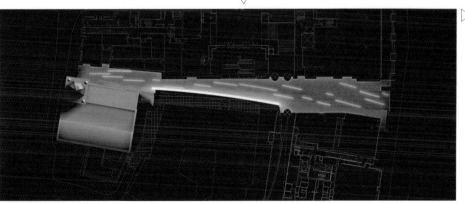

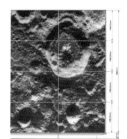

Elevations and section of glass screen

0614

0614 Querkraft created a unique, high-interest feature for the city of Vienna, Austria. A long frame elevated 9 feet (2.7 m) above the ground provides illuminated advertising space that doubles as a taxi stand and bus stop. Below, glow-in-the-dark seating creates a cozy outdoor living room protected by glass panels with printed plant motifs.

0615 With the Norwegian pavilion for Shanghai Expo 2010, architects Helen & Hard explored the topic of sustainable urban development using materials such as laminated bamboo and ETFE textile. The most memorable feature was the northern lights shows staged on the roof of the pavilion via projection.

0616 The lighting scheme designed by Roger Narboni for Chartres' town center not only beautifies the streets, enhancing the French city's architectural heritage, but it also resolves the issue of usually dark and unsafe parking garages, bringing them to life with theatrical light.

0615

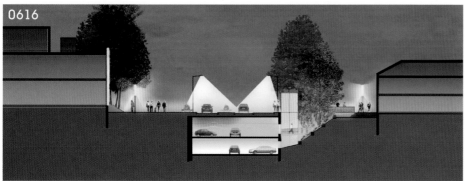

0616

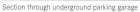
Section through underground parking garage

0617 The southern railway track in the city area of Graz, Austria, is characterized by 13 underpasses. As a result of the different levels of railway tracks and bicycle and foot paths, terraces were created. Careful plant combinations ensure a smooth transition between levels, and the different colors help people navigate through the different areas.

0618 Rudolf Bechar Park occupies the site previously occupied by a train station. Hager Landschaftsarchitektur used this as an opportunity to transform the railroad tracks into planting beds.

0619 Aguasverdes Park responds to the limitations of water shortages by using treated sewage water to amend the soil on the site for gardens, field, and forests and to irrigate non-food plantings.

0620 Rudolf Bechar Park is located in a gentrified neighborhood of Vienna, Austria. The "veil of trees" oriented to the nearby Danube River delimits the space and divides it into different zones.

A. WOOD RIDGE
   Pinus, Quercus, Juniperus
B. WOODED CRESTS
   Pinus, Quercus, Juniperus
C. DRY GROVES
   Olea, Prunus (almond)
D. ORGANIC MIGRANTS
   Arbutus, Quercus coccifera, Q. suber
E. UPLAND MEADOW
   Lavandula, Retama, Retama, Phyllirea
F. PLANT AND PLAY PLINTHS
   Ficus, Punica, Prunus (plum and cherry)
G. RIPARIAN SPONGE
   Fraxinus, Populus, Ulmus, Alnus, Salix, Tamarix
H. GREENWATER TRAYS
   Reeds, sedges, rushes
I. URBAN STRAND
   Robinia, Aesculus, Gleditsia, Melia

Vegetation plan

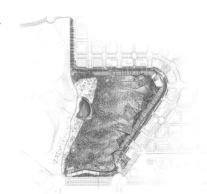

Master plan

0621

0622

0621 Imchenplatz Berlin-Spandau, in Germany, is an example of landscape architects Glasser und Dagenbach's expertise in the creation of open public spaces and the reconstruction of existing parks and gardens.

0622 With Tanner Springs, a park in Portland, Oregon, Atelier Dreiseitl succeeds in recapturing the area's past with its native wetlands.

0623 RMP Stephan Lenzen integrated artwork within the landscape, which, through the seasons, continuously transforms the Dyck Field in Jüchen, Germany.

0624 The Floating Gardens is a park along the Yongning River in Taizhou City, China. Turenscape's approach was that of a park that incorporates minimum design techniques and introduces wetlands and local vegetation designed for the natural processes of flooding.

0623

0624

0625

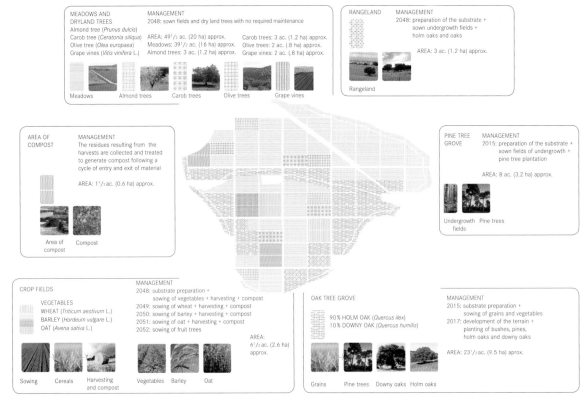

MEADOWS AND DRYLAND TREES
Almond tree (*Prunus dulcis*)
Carob tree (*Ceratonia siliqua*)
Olive tree (*Olea europaea*)
Grape vines (*Vitis vinifera* L.)

MANAGEMENT
2048: sown fields and dry land trees with no required maintenance

AREA: 49¹/₂ ac. (20 ha) approx.
Meadows: 39¹/₂ ac. (16 ha) approx.
Almond trees: 3 ac. (1.2 ha) approx.

Carob trees: 3 ac. (1.2 ha) approx.
Olive trees: 2 ac. (.8 ha) approx.
Grape vines: 2 ac. (.8 ha) approx.

Meadows   Almond trees   Carob trees   Olive trees   Grape vines

RANGELAND   MANAGEMENT
2048: preparation of the substrate + sown undergrowth fields + holm oaks and oaks

AREA: 3 ac. (1.2 ha) approx.

Rangeland

AREA OF COMPOST   MANAGEMENT
The residues resulting from the harvests are collected and treated to generate compost following a cycle of entry and exit of material

AREA: 1¹/₂ ac. (0.6 ha) approx.

Area of compost   Compost

PINE TREE GROVE   MANAGEMENT
2015: preparation of the substrate + sown fields of undergrowth + pine tree plantation

AREA: 8 ac. (3.2 ha) approx.

Undergrowth fields   Pine trees

CROP FIELDS

VEGETABLES
WHEAT (*Triticum aestivum* L.)
BARLEY (*Hordeum vulgare* L.)
OAT (*Avena sativa* L.)

MANAGEMENT
2048: substrate preparation + sowing of vegetables + harvesting + compost
2049: sowing of wheat + harvesting + compost
2050: sowing of barley + harvesting + compost
2051: sowing of oat + harvesting + compost
2052: sowing of fruit trees

AREA: 6¹/₂ ac. (2.6 ha) approx.

Sowing   Cereals   Harvesting and compost   Vegetables   Barley   Oat

OAK TREE GROVE

90% HOLM OAK (*Quercus ilex*)
10% DOWNY OAK (*Quercus humilis*)

MANAGEMENT
2015: substrate preparation + sowing of grains and vegetables
2017: development of the terrain + planting of bushes, pines, holm oaks and downy oaks

AREA: 23¹/₂ ac. (9.5 ha) aprox.

Grains   Pine trees   Downy oaks   Holm oaks

Vegetation and crops diagram for 2048

0626

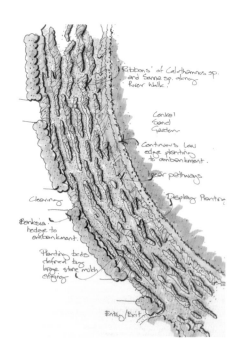

Ribbons' of Calothamnus sp. and Senna sp. along River Walk

Central Sand Garden

Continuous Low edge planting to embankment

Linear pathways

Display Planting

Clearings

Banksia hedge to embankment

Planting beds deflect turns large stone mulch edging

Entry/Exit

Detailed plan of the garden

0627

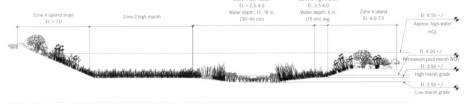

| Zone 4 upland slope El. > 7.0 | Zone-2 high marsh | Zone 1 low marsh El. > 2.5-4.0 Water depth: 12-18 in. (30-46 cm) | Zone 2 high marsh El. 3.5-4.0 Water depth: 6 in. (15 cm) avg. | Zone 4 island El. 4.0-7.5 |

El. 8.50 +/- Approx. high-water HGL

El. 4.00 +/- Permanent pool marsh WUV
El. 3.50 +/- High marsh grade

El. 2.50 +/- Low marsh grade

Typical marsh planting zone section

0628

0629

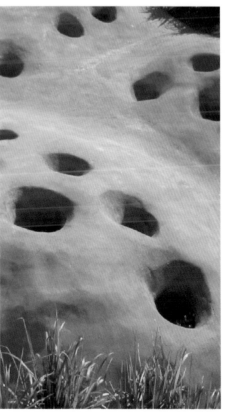

0625 The Uniland Quarry project in Olèrdola, Spain, proposed by aldayjover arquitectura y paisaje, is an attempt to integrate an abandoned quarry into the rich agricultural environment that characterizes the region.

0626 Located in Cranbourne, Australia, the Australian Garden is a division of the Royal Botanic Gardens in Melbourne. It features about 100,000 plants distributed across 15 landscape displays and exhibition gardens.

0627 Pacific Commons is emblematic of CMG Landscape Architecture's unique approach to complex system-based landscapes that combine infrastructure with ecological and water-quality functions.

0628 The waterfront presents different possibilities in the way cities deal with water. To emphasize the link between the city of Doesburg in the Netherlands and its river, Okra's design harmoniously adapts to the changes due to the natural processes of flooding.

0629 LAND-I developed the landscape of Cornerstone Gardens around the idea of enlarging the scale of a stone to the point that it becomes a landscape. Planted holes in the stone are "life pockets" in the otherwise inert material.

0630 Highlight Munich Business Towers constitute a high-rise ensemble in Munich, Germany. Rainer Schmidt Landschaftsarchitekten developed a design for the outdoor space of this complex that is distinguished by circular forms. These appear in planted hills, planters and paved areas of concentric circles.

0630

0631 The Sensational Garden in Frosinone, Italy, is an open space made of five different areas, which are metaphors for each of the five human senses. Nabito Architects & Partners succeeded in creating a stimulating environment with aromatic plants, trees and flowers.

0632 The Tanghe River through Qinhuangdao, China is the setting for the Red Ribbon, a minimalist intervention developed by Turenscape. The Red Ribbon, which spans 547 yards (500 m), is made of steel fiber and various plants grow in strategically placed holes.

0633 The garden in the lobby of the New York Times Building emphasizes a poetic approach that references the Hudson River Valley woodland landscape. A study of the growing conditions was critical to determine species selection, arrangement and planting to ensure long-term sustainability.

0634 SLA created an urban space to tie the new headquarters of the Swedish SEB Bank with its surrounding area in Copenhagen. The trees and herbaceous borders are planted in fissures between the white concrete slabs that form the roof of a parking structure.

0631

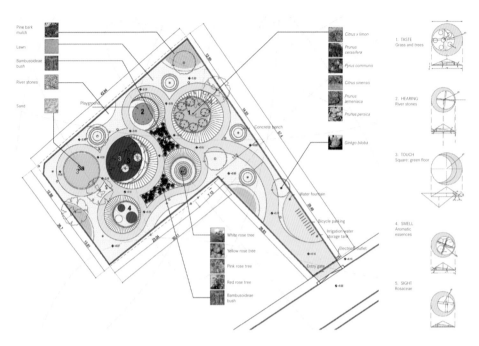

Site plan of the park

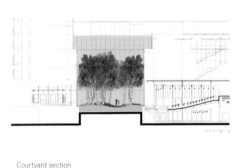

Courtyard section

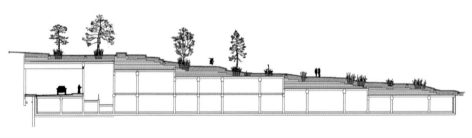

Section through square above parking structure

0635 More and more hotels are converting their roof terraces into gardens that offer more than just plant and flower arrangements. Many have embraced the farm-to-table concept and are growing their own herbs, vegetables and fruits.

0636 Architectural details add character to an outdoor space in the same way that plants can make an architectural and artistic statement.

0637 Rock gardens are not simply designed to imitate native plants growing in natural stone outcroppings. They can enhance any kind of planting area, from perennial rock garden plants to desert settings with cacti and succulents.

0638 For the Center for Ideas of the Victorian College of the Arts in Melbourne, Australia, Rush Wright Associates created a landscape derived from the nested geometry of a hexagon. This geometry was extended across the site and served to create seating, plinths and planting beds. Such powerful hardscape required a very minimal planting intervention.

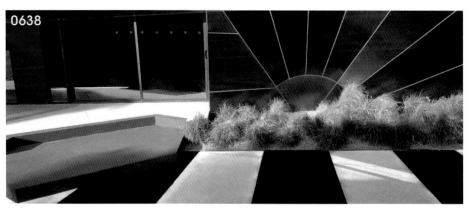

0639 Plants and vegetation are ever-changing. What we need is a comprehensive maintenance strategy to ensure that the images and conditions the design concept has been based on can be achieved in the short and long term.

0640 The southern railway track in Graz, Austria, is formed by various underpasses. Terraces were connected from each level of path to the next by plant combinations to ensure a smooth transition.

0641 The abstraction and reinterpretation of existing features are the base on which the design approach is built on. For the Peneder project designed by 3:0 Landschaftsarchitektur, the principles that compose the design have been taken from the surrounding cultural landscape.

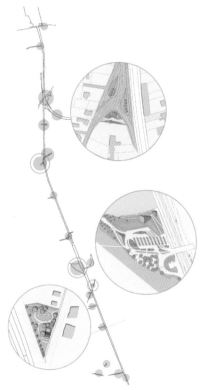

0641

 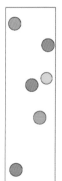

Site plan of the underpasses

Planting design diagrams

Site plan

0642

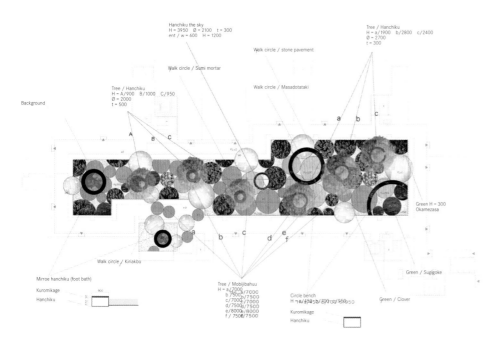

Hanchiku the sky
H = 3950   Ø = 2100   t = 300
ent / w = 600   H = 1200

Walk circle / stone pavement

Walk circle / Sumi mortar

Tree / Hanchiku
H = a/1900   b/2800   c/2400
Ø = 2700
t = 300

Walk circle / Masadotataki

Tree / Hanchiku
H = A/900   B/1000   C/950
Ø = 2000
t = 500

Background

Green H = 300
Okamezasa

Walk circle / Kiriakbu

Green / Sugigoke

Mirroe hanchiku (foot bath)

Kuromikage

Hanchiku

Tree / Mobijibahuu
H = a /7000
b /7500 b /7000
c /7000 c /7000
d /7500 d /7500
e /8000 e /8000
f / 7500 f /7500

Circle bench
H = a/450 b /700 c /950
Kuromikage
Hanchiku

Green / Clover

Site plan

0643

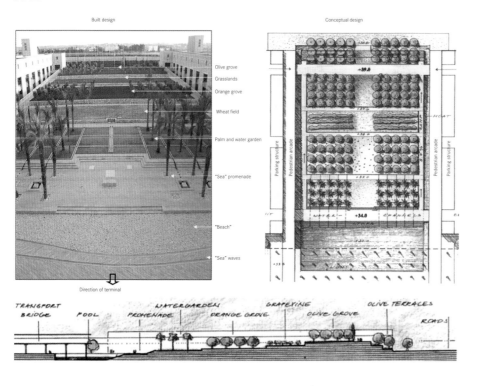

Built design

Conceptual design

Olive grove
Grasslands
Orange grove

Wheat field

Palm and water garden

"Sea" promenade

"Beach"

"Sea" waves

+39.0

Parking structure

Pedestrian arcade

Pedestrian arcade

Parking structure

Direction of terminal

TRANSPORT BRIDGE   POOL   WATERGARDEN PROMENADE   ORANGE GROVE   GRAPEVINE   OLIVE GROVE   OLIVE TERRACES   ROADS

0642 This garden project is at the main station in Yamagata City, Japan. This design by 1moku co. derives from their interpretation of the Mogami River's flowing patterns.

0643 The landscape design of Ben Gurion International Airport by Barbara Aronson relates strongly to the surrounding landscape of citrus groves and agricultural fields from the coastal plain around Tel Aviv, Israel, up to the mountains of Jerusalem.

0644 In the planting scheme for the Chorinerstrasse residential courtyard in Berlin, 100 Landschaftsarchitektur only used three plant species, based on their texture and changing color: the blue filigree foliage of festuca, the thick red-green leaf flaps of bergenia and the copper-bright upright stems of calamagrostis.

0645 Plants are one of the main elements of the landscape design for the Olimia Hotel in Podčetrtek, Slovenia. Knowledge about plants can help us solve technical problems. The extensive planting for the hotel was carried out on extreme slopes, in some parts up to 70 degrees.

0644

0645

0646 A large concrete planting bed ties the architectural style of the adjacent building in with the street paving. The trees offer a splash of color that changes with the seasons.

0647 A new British Embassy in Yemen is located in the diplomatic district of Sana'a, near the base of the mountains, where the climate is intensely dry with periodic heavy rainfall in the short rainy season. The landscape strategy was defined by the need to create shelter within the site to reduce exposure from prevailing winds and to mitigate soil loss.

0648 The rationalist architecture contrasts with the organic presence of a single tree planted in a large square tree well placed at the center of a courtyard.

0649 The Jardin Paul Eluard in Mantes-la-Ville, France, presents massive groups of leafy plants near water (partially shaded) that articulate the trails along the river. The office of Collin Paysage used a simple vocabulary of gabions and soil stabilization associated with the natural landscape.

0650 Technical solutions and materials should age well. It takes years to reach the planned state. Materials and technical solutions must support the aging process, for example, with patina.

0651 Plants are always in motion. Next to regarding seasonal and lifelong changes, the question of continuous care of green spaces must be considered. Only well-kept green spaces reach the design's aim.

0652 What is built and what is planted form the places of public life. Large trees can match the size and volume of buildings. The rows of trees echo the lines of the buildings and articulate the different blocks.

0653 When preparing your planting scheme, always think about simplicity, unity, harmony, balance and scale. Combining attractive yet contrasting leaf forms and textures helps you obtain a distinct and remarkable image.

0646

0647

0648

0649

0650

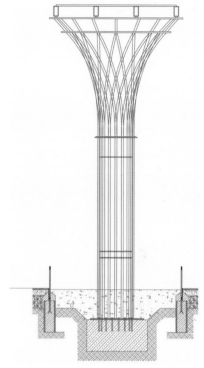

Section through trellis column

0651

0652

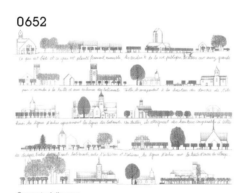

Conceptual diagram

0653

0654 While the "bones" of a garden are formed by plants that provide structure and give the landscape interest even in the dim days of winter, secondary plants contribute to seasonal interest, texture and rhythm.

0655 For Barrel Warehouse Park in Waterloo, Canada, Janet Rosenberg was inspired by the site's historical identity as the setting for grain distilleries and barrel warehouses. The scheme included ornamental grasses to suggest fields of grains and incorporated large industrial artifacts as art pieces that pay tribute to the industrial heritage of the city.

0656 Natural plantings make the site more hospitable. Planting design coordinates solar orientation and wind protection for optimum use. Hedgerow trees and shrubs create a green corridor that provides shade and protection from the wind for park users while serving as a wildflower corridor.

0657 Annuals are often the star performers that contribute to the seasonal interest of a garden. Each plant offers its unique character, often resulting in a display of color that looks more carefully designed that it actually was.

0658

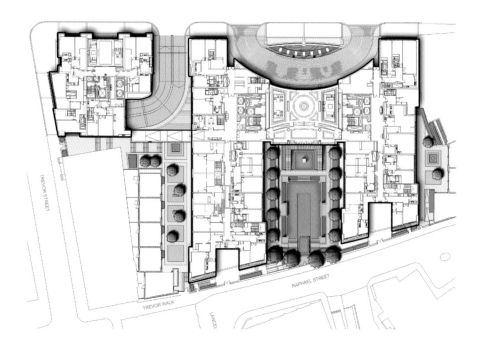

Site plan

▽

0658 In an urban development, the landscape should reflect and respect the aesthetic of the surrounding architecture. Here the landscape boasts a sleek modern perspective that emphasizes the simple, elegant nature of the building.

0659 The selection of plants forms a key element in defining the future identity of the space. Plants will continue to change in color, sound and scent throughout the season. Based on the landscape setting of the space, the placing and choice of plants need to be specific to the particularities of the site.

0660 The most memorable landscapes are stimulating and profoundly sensual. Try to keep in mind the effects that sounds, water movements and people create in a space. Play with textured plants, from soft lamb's ears (*Stachys byzantia*) to spiky euphorbias.

0661 For the surroundings of the Harley-Davidson Museum in Milwaukee, Wisconsin, oslund.and.assoc. chose plant materials to reintroduce the riparian landscape of the Menomonee River Valley. These included prairie forbs and grasses native to the region.

0659

0660

0661

0662 These grass terraces around a property in Hillsborough, California, show that a limited plant palette often achieves a striking plant design. Shades of Green Landscape Architecture created bands of plants focusing on subtle color changes and texture.

0663 In dry climates, one of the most important things we can do for the environment is to use drought-tolerant plants. This saves the cost of installing an irrigation system and reduces maintenance by eliminating weeding in the summer and reducing pests.

0664 For this site on the Greek island of Aegina, planting adapted to the long summer drought was necessary so that the landscape appears to merge with the natural surroundings.

0665 Local plants and stone selected from a local quarry were used to tie the terraces of the land into the steps and terraces around this house at Epidravros, Greece. Formal gardens were kept to a minimum for amenity and utility and to enjoy the natural landscape.

0666

0668

0667

0666 Simple materials and a limited selection of plants were used for the award-winning Grace boutique hotel overlooking the spectacular Caldera of Santorini, Greece. Six months of drought, the hot, dry, salt-laden Meltemi wind and the Mediterranean sun make this a tough environment, which conditioned the design.

0667 Offset lush informal planting against architectural elements to energize the space. At Icon Office Development, stainless steel, water and granite were juxtaposed against the movement and color variation provided by *Calamagrostis*, *Stipa* and various flowering perennials.

0668 This landscape provides the natural forecourt and front window for a furniture showroom on the national road through mountainous northern Greece. A path cuts a tilted plane of grass and lavender.

0669 A 62-acre (25 ha) site located within City Park in New Orleans, Louisiana, was the object of a plan for reestablishing the ecosystem and halting the spread of invasive species on the site. Planting of native seeds and plants along with continued invasive species management over the first 5-10 years gave the ecosystem a chance to re-establish itself.

0670 On this site, 75% of the plant materials are native to the Cabo San Lucas region. Many of the unique plants were collected in the nearby desert, at a site where a landfill was being constructed and the plants being destroyed. Today the native Baja plants are the highlight of Las Ventanas garden.

0671 A pool and water feature act as an axis, connecting the entrance of a property with the house while organizing various ornamental, herb and vegetable gardens.

0669

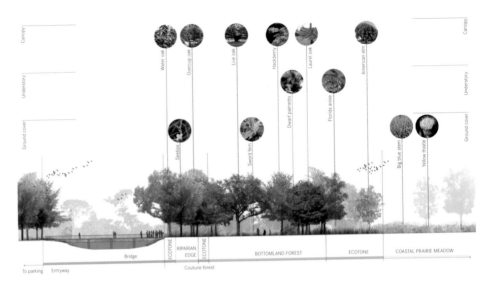

Diagram of the recreation of a multi-storied canopy

0671

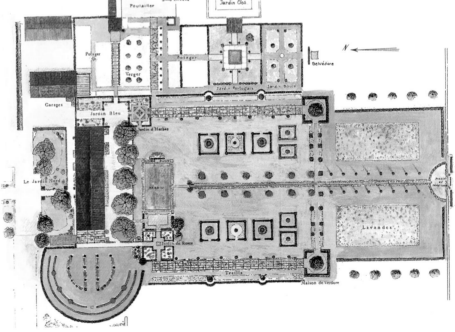

Site plan

0672 A lush but controlled planting scheme offsets the strong geometric form of the fountains and provides softness and a sense of scale, elevating this secluded garden above the ordinary.

0673 Adaptive vegetation communities dot the regional landscape in patches. Sensitive to water and soil pH values and able to dig cavities of various depths, they can create diverse environmental conditions to initiate the processes of adaptation.

0674 The rice paddy campus of Shenyang Jianzhu University, China, by Turenscape is a reinterpretation of the traditional Chinese rice growing culture and an example of a productive landscape.

0675 Selection of plants should be in accordance with the specific location and exposure to sun and wind. This leads to grouping plants with similar requirements, building the architecture of the site in terms of geometry, proportion, size and rhythm.

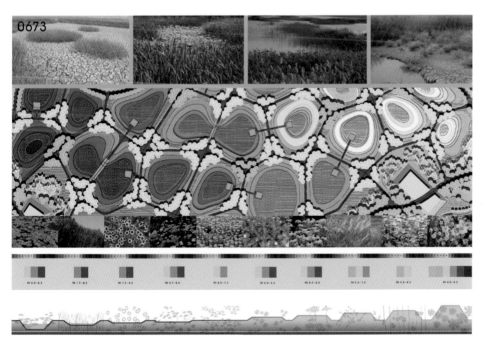

Plan and section diagrams of adaptive vegetation communities

0676

0677

0678

0679

0676 The design of this roof terrace is proof that green roof agriculture is viable as an urban agricultural alternative. Stylish yet casual and intimate, an herb garden on a rooftop mixes aesthetics with culinary applications.

0677 Ferns with big leaves and tall grasses such as bamboo help create secluded spots, thus avoiding additional construction and blurring the boundaries between architecture and nature, interior and exterior.

0678 Climbing plants such as rose, jasmine, clematis, grape, or bougainvillea can be used to cover a wall or a fence. Some need vertical support, others horizontal support, and others no support at all.

0679 Although flowers in Japanese gardens are not common, it has not always been rare to find them in this type of setting. During the Heian Period (794-1185) they were planted in spectacular gardens.

0680 Jasmine and bougainvillea can be very effective to cover a wall between roof terraces and create vertical gardens. The beauty of blooming climbing plants cannot be denied, and some produce spectacular flower displays.

0681 The plant selection was made based on the site's climatic conditions and has 37 different species of succulent plants. During the summer, these plants improve the air quality and lower the temperature of the building's light wells, where they have been planted.

0682 Drip irrigation is the most effective method to maintain a garden. Thanks to a humidity sensor that detects rain or moisture in the soil, it only works when it is necessary. Before thinking about the type of irrigation that uses the least amount of water, it is first necessary to select plants that live on little water.

0683 A compartmentalized garden makes the most of a small outdoor space around a house. Placing vegetables, herbs and ornamental plants next to each other is a good way to hinder insects and diseases. For example, plant garlic next to roses to repel aphids, and plant asters around asparagus to discourage pests.

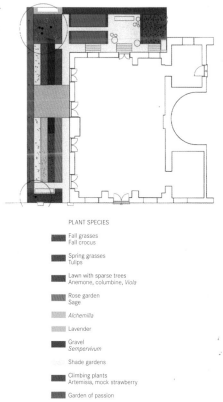

PLANT SPECIES

Fall grasses
Fall crocus

Spring grasses
Tulips

Lawn with sparse trees
Anemone, columbine, *Viola*

Rose garden
Sage

Alchemilla

Lavender

Gravel
Sempervivum

Shade gardens

Climbing plants
Artemisia, mock strawberry

Garden of passion

0684

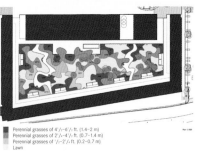
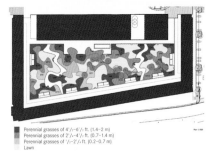

■ Perennial grasses of 4¹/₂–6¹/₂ ft. (1.4–2 m)
■ Perennial grasses of 2¹/₂–4¹/₂ ft. (0.7–1.4 m)
□ Perennial grasses of ¹/₂–2¹/₂ ft. (0.2–0.7 m)
□ Lawn

Site plan

0685

0686

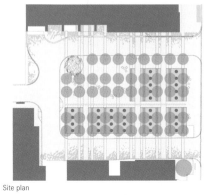

Site plan

0687

0688

Site plan

0689

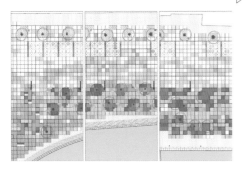

Partial promenade pavement plan

Garden study

0684 The plants define the different spaces that constitute Charlotte Garden in Copenhagen, Denmark, designed by SLA. Plantings primarily consist of different grasses, such as blue fescue, Balkan blue grass and purple moor.

0685 Large planted areas have a cooling effect on their surroundings, thus reducing the stress produced by the heat island. Studies made on clear nights with light wind show that Chapultepec Park in Mexico City is 3.6–5.4°F (2–3°C) cooler within its boundaries.

0686 Janet Rosenberg + Associates modeled the Town Hall Square in Toronto, Canada, after the French parterre. Some of the eye-catching elements among the vegetation are the large planters and the box-like hedges aligned with the pattern of the pavement.

0687 The architects gave much importance to the vegetation so as to create a strong natural atmosphere within the urban fabric.

0688 Delta Vorm Groep designed a terraced garden with low plants and sparse trees between two newly constructed buildings in Utrecht, the Netherlands. The design is characterized by broken lines that connect the two buildings.

0689 Hager Landschaftsarchitektur designed the exterior space around a residential complex in Zurich, Switzerland, where rows of plane trees separate the garden from the nearby busy streets, and circular grass patches connect the different buildings while creating rhythm.

0690 3LHD developed a comprehensive change to the layout of the waterfront of Split in Croatia with the objective of reinvigorating commercial and recreational activity. Plants were chosen for their color and shape and were planted on one side of the promenade. They are mostly short so as not to interfere with the seascape.

0691 Set in a formal French style, these hedges are elegantly trimmed to form pleasant patterns, while the white gravel and the tree recall Japanese gardens. Surprisingly, both styles combine to form an attractive "Zen parterre."

0692 The nicely trimmed hedges create a landscape of rolling mounds. This is the approach that Glasser und Dagenbach adopted for the remodel of the Garten von Ehren in Hamburg, Germany.

0693 The open spaces around the Infineon Asia Pacific Headquarters designed by GTL feature continuous slate pavement with different elements, including benches and planters in one.

0694 The expertise of the landscape architecture office of Glasser und Dagenbach is evident in their renovation and redesign of historic parks. An example of this is the Imchenplatz Berlin-Spandau, Germany, where the designers introduced boat-shaped planters in reference to the sea and the maritime tradition of the city.

0695 The garden of a modernist villa in Vilnius, Lithuania, presents examples of the most characteristic elements of Glasser und Dagenbach. The designers created spectacular geometric sculptures, half made of granite, half made of hedges.

0696 Inspired by Zen gardens, the design of Vilnius Villa's grounds is an environment that takes advantage of certain plant forms, which are used to divide different zones.

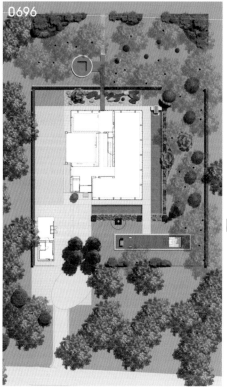

Site plan

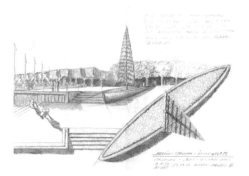

Artist's impression

0697

Roof plan

▷

0697 The object of this renovation by Burger Land-schaftsarchitekten was to find a unifying theme for a group of buildings in Unterföhring, a neighborhood in Munich, Germany. The design centers on two levels: the first is at street-level, where the spaces between buildings are paved with stone, and the second affects the rooftops, which are covered with gardens.

0698 The pavement of the spaces between the buildings is composed of dolomite stone slabs and grass and contrasts with the rigidity of the urban fabric.

0699 For the backyard of a private residence in San Francisco, California, Lundberg Design created a rhythmic sequence of low black stone walls and a thin white border that alternates with elongated flower beds.

0698

0699

Site plan

0700 The courtyard of a residential complex in Montreal, Canada, offers planting beds along the perimeter and large gabions planted with hedges to mark accesses to the buildings.

0701 Promenade of Light by Tonkin Liu is the result of the renewal of a promenade in London, England, whose concept is based on a circular element and its different possibilities of use, such as tree wells, benches and planting beds.

0702 Laurentian flora was a temporary installation on the grounds of the historic monastery of Padua, Italy. NIPpaysage created large spheres as a metaphor for seeds that could grow a selection of plants and produce a novel herbarium.

0703 For the Sampling Gardens in Tianjing, China, Turenscape designed diverse habitats where the natural process of plant adaptation and community evolution were initiated to transform a former garbage dump into a low-maintenance urban park.

0704

0704 Mosbach Paysagistes' Botanical Garden of Bordeaux in France is characterized by the dynamics of its landscape. It is laid out around six spaces devoted to different types of cultivation.

0705 In the context of an event that presented gardening novelties, NIPpaysage created Green Shift. Both a garden and a playground, the site emerges as a sculptural landscape that combines vegetation and manufactured products.

0706 LAND-I created Ombre for a gardening festival in Grand-Métis, Canada. Reference to a necropolis is strong, but one soon discovers that the ground at the bottom of the pits is covered with low-growing plants.

0707 The Australian Garden in Cranbourne features the diversity of Australian flora that has evolved to adapt to the climatic variations that the continent offers.

0705

Site plan

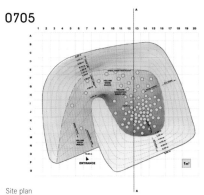

0706

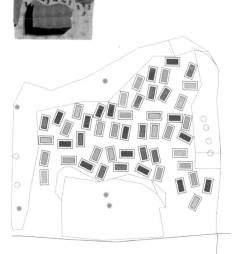

Site plan

0707

0708 The mag.MA architetture studio named their restoration of the Matteotti Square in Badalucco, Italy, Craquelure. The name makes reference to the cracking of dried mud in the sun. But, in fact, theses cracks are wide planting beds that allow the olive trees, so characteristic of the region's landscape, to regain possession of the place.

0709 A large landscape development along the Manzanares River in Madrid, Spain, offers botanical variety, creating different atmospheres in the artificial leas and allowing a clear structuring of the spaces.

0710 An outdoor learning courtyard for the Natural Sciences Department at Keene State College, New Hampshire, is linked to the school's curriculum, providing a model outdoor field laboratory to promote botanical and horticultural awareness to both the college and the community.

Site plan

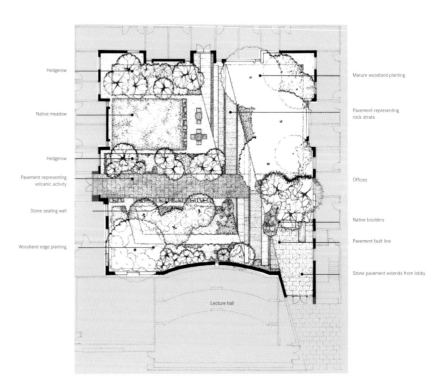

Hedgerow

Native meadow

Hedgerow

Pavement representing volcanic activity

Stone seating wall

Woodland edge planting

Mature woodland planting

Pavement representing rock strata

Offices

Native boulders

Pavement fault line

Stone pavement extends from lobby

Lecture hall

Site plan

0711

0711 The arboretum at Klangenfurt Hospital is specially tailored to the tree species collection of the institution. Various courtyards imbue the complex with green. The colors of the leaves and blooms of each plant specimen influenced the color of the undergrowth and ground covering.

0712 The texture of the bark of each species of tree was a source of inspiration for the arrangement and shape of the terraces and planting troughs.

0713 The open architecture with long glass windows creates close interaction between interior and exterior spaces. The choice of plants is based on their healing properties, taking into account harmful allergens.

0712

0713

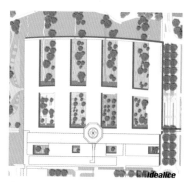

Site plan

0714

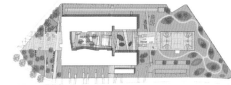

Site plan

0715

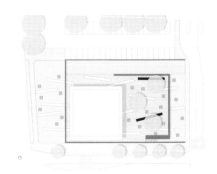

0716

Site plan

0714 Idealice designed the open spaces around Contiweg Secondary School in Vienna, Austria. Trees were planted to provide structure to the free space and, at the same time, to offer a learning pathway.

0715 For the Vienna Airport Tower Square, the idea of contrasting pairs is the central theme: light versus dark, and smooth versus textured. Rust-colored Corten steel planting beds seem to grow out of the gravel, adding another layer of texture and color.

0716 The Courtyard in the Wind by Acconci Studio is an example of how architecture affects landscape and vice versa. In the courtyard, a turntable is cut in the lawn and the pavement; up in the tower, a wind turbine rotates, capturing wind energy to power the turntable of the landscape.

0717

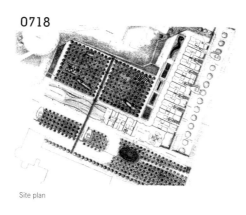

0718

Site plan

0719

0717 1moku co. planned the rooftop garden of the Shanghai Grand Theater, China, taking into consideration the history of the building and its Art Deco style.

0718 A sense of fun and pleasure is captured in a field of fruit trees with rich, dense underplanting. Within the orchard are "secret" gardens, spaces for people to reflect and pause. The long water rill of brilliant color translates the river into the orchard.

0719 In this urban public space directly adjacent to the street, all the planting is at ground level with no delimiting edges and planters typical of the modernist landscape vernacular. With their design of Place Ville Marie, Cardinal Hardy wanted to offer an image representative of modern Montreal (Canada).

0720 The concept of urban park space goes beyond the idea of a natural haven. It also is an attraction and a site for entertainment. An example of such a design concept is the arrangement that Bruto Landscape Architecture designed for the vast shopping area BTC in the city of Ljubljana, Slovenia

0721 3:0 Landschaftsarchitektur designed a new playground in Altenmarkt in the Pongau Region of the Austrian Alps, where the steep topography dictates the layout of the project. The playground's main attraction is the green terrain itself.

0720

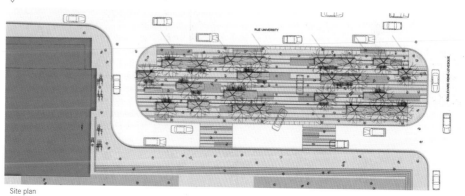

Site plan

0721

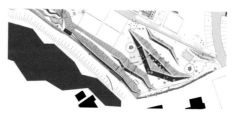

Site plan

0722 The master planning and landscape project for a private estate in Jurmala on the Gulf of Riga, Latvia, is set in a pine forest. The minimal intervention of neatly trimmed hedges forming geometric forms is completed with the client's collection of modern and historic sculptures.

0723 This development in Fulham, West London, England, is a mix of new and existing housing, office and retail space and restaurants. The first-floor dry garden, planted with palms, yuccas, cordylines and agave, provides a communal space for the residents and office workers who share the space.

0724 The Recoleta Cultural Center in Buenos Aires, Argentina, includes a butterfly garden that is active for 6 months each year. This ephemeral setting brings visitors closer to the charm of butterflies which are so hard to find in cities and tries to raise awareness about urban biodiversity.

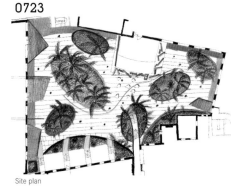

Site plan

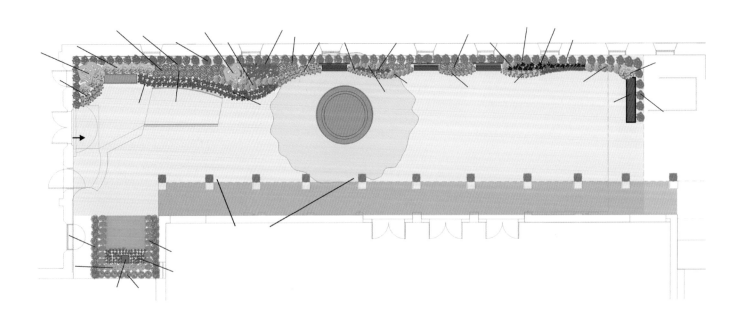

Plan of the Summer Butterfly Garden

0725

0725 Buildings and landscapes must be conceived as sensitive and interesting compositions of natural and man-made elements. Form, function and materials should blend into seamless environments where buildings and landscapes live together in mutual respect.

0726 Recreational landscapes provide exciting opportunities to inspire children's creativity and physical development. Creative playgrounds provide direct contact between the children and nature and should be designed to stimulate the senses by using natural textures, forms, and materials in interesting ways.

0727 This innovative design for a former water purification site combines the use of woods for a slow process of natural purification with an experimental approach to forestry. By mixing species of different sizes and in different numbers, this young forest, a few years after planting, already feels like an established woods.

0726

0727

Site plan

0728 The character of a landscape is defined by its edges and boundaries. The "border" is an ancient concept as fundamental in today's landscape design as it was in antiquity. The plantings are organized in a rhythmic composition that mixes height, texture and color and, at the same time, solves the basic slope stabilization on the site.

0729 Vegetation structures the space.

0730 Alter Botanischer Garten is a historical downtown park in Munich, Germany, that was reshaped in the context of an urban redevelopment. The wooded areas, which after years of neglect have reverted to an almost natural state, contrast well with the formal plantings at the center of the park.

0731 An inexpensive way to make any landscape more dynamic is through interesting topography. The site of Barrel Warehouse Park in Waterloo, Canada, was an ordinary streetscape. Janet Rosenberg + Associates created sculpted lawns that add dimension and playfulness in the form of rolling hills.

0732 Landscapes are compositions of views extending far beyond the boundaries of individual sites. Simple transformations of boundary lines into landscape edges can achieve a dramatic sense of infinity.

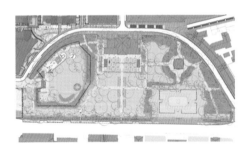

Site plan

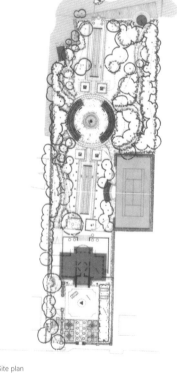

Site plan

0733

0733 The design of this small park in Utrecht, the Netherlands, is a green oasis in the city. Despite the reduced dimensions of the area, the park exudes spaciousness thanks to various green mounds that act as independent islands.

0734 Lodewijk Baljon Landscape Architects designed the front yards of the Pothoofd Apartments in Deventer, the Netherlands, in the French garden style. Repetition lessens the uniqueness of an element but creates rhythm and provides the setting with depth.

0735 Landlab was involved in the renovation of the grounds around this monument in the shape of a pyramid topped by an obelisk and in the creation of the stairs to it. Called the Pyramid of Austerlitz, it commemorates the French occupation of the Netherlands.

0736 Aerdenhout Garden in the Netherlands, by Lodewijk Baljon Landscape Architects, responds to the idea of "conceptual garden," which is based on the architectural character of landscaping. Tim Richardson, a landscape writer and critic, states that this style "is a way of adding richness, meaning and emotion to a design."

0737 Hedges structure spaces with their sculptural character. They create a solid background for a display of other garden elements, such as water features and other plant species, or take center stage in creative topiary designs.

0734

0735

0736

0737

0738 The strong, flowing columbarium passages of Willamette National Cemetery's expansion transforms a steep, open field into a place that mutually respects human needs and the natural environment. It reverses the inward-focus of traditional cemetery architecture by embracing forested surroundings and off-site landscapes.

0739 Designed landscapes at Nike World Headquarters in Beaverton, Oregon, combine the stunning outdoor spaces with enhanced water quality sites and habitats. The calm and beauty of the natural world inspires athletes, employees and visitors alike.

0740 The daily workplace can be engaging, inspirational and rewarding thanks to well-designed outdoor spaces with abundant vegetation. Create flexible, social outdoor spaces where we collaborate, share our lives, dine, enjoy one another and relieve stress.

0741 The most cost-effective element of the project, the planting, can have the boldest effect. Don't underestimate the power of plants to intrigue and engage people in urban spaces.

0742

0742 Large expanses of the same plant species reinforce the idea that sometimes landscape is strongest when it's simple. The fewer design moves there are, the larger a landscape tends to feel. Planting in masses emulates nature, where it is easy to find large communities of a single plant species.

0743 Whether big or small, a garden layout should adopt a clear principle, whether it is static or dynamic, and always take orientation into account.

0744 Growth retardants include subsurface materials. For the design of Not Garden, PEG office of landscape + architecture used laser-cutter fabrication to cut circles out of geotextile (a weed-control barrier)

0743

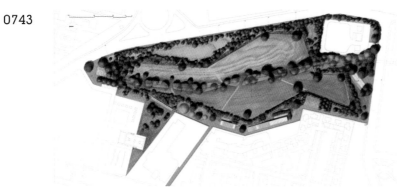

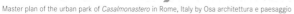

Master plan of the urban park of *Casalmonastero* in Rome, Italy by Osa architettura e paesaggio

0744

0745 While landscape architecture is mostly perceived as a brilliant combination of creative engineering work and the craft of horticulture, some may think of it as art.

0746 The introduction of planted roofs to the striking forms of contemporary architecture was quickly embraced because of the broad-ranging environmental benefits of this innovative system.

0747 Consider grouping plants with similar light, soil and water requirements together. Native plants minimize the need for water and fertilizer.

0748 The IADT campus concept developed by Stephen Diamond Associates is as an abstract composition formed by *Calamagrostis* intersected by strips of flowering perennials to channel views and integrate the campus into its context.

0749

0750

0751

0749 SWA was hired by Lite-On, a major Taiwanese electronics company, to design its new corporate headquarters on a site overlooking the Gee Long River. The result is a 25-story slender tower rising above a sloped landscape podium. A light well opens to a courtyard below, providing the cafeteria at the lower level with garden views.

0750 Verakin is a central component of Chongqing's new Tea Garden District. SWA provided the inhabitants of a community with open spaces. The different areas are thoughtfully located to enhance accessibility and visibility.

0751 The design of SGI campus (Google's headquarters) and the adjacent Charleston Park in Mountain View, California, creates a strong identity for the campus and provides a much-needed civic space. The contemplative East Garden's circular mounds echo the Calaveros Hills, seen in the distance beyond.

0752 Landscape architect Birk Nielsen of Sweco created a pleasant and functional garden to be enjoyed. It is also a beautiful courtyard that can be admired from the apartments around it.

0752

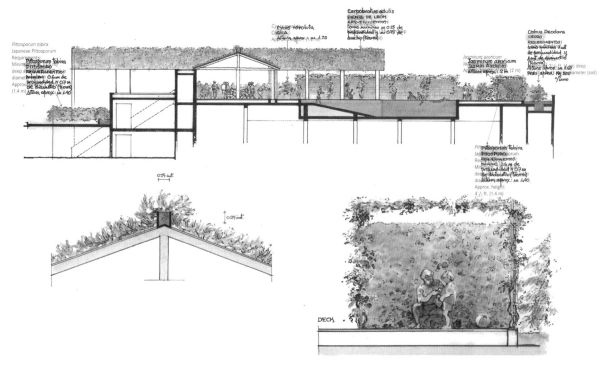

Section through pool, roof and deck (with details)

0753 Scale is particularly important when designing the exterior of a building. The sizes of the plant specimens selected should harmonize with the structure.

0754 Vacant plots' weeds are important elements of the urban ecosystem and here, in a project called Topographical Amnesias, were taken as the main element of the landscape design. Urban voids are a way to rethink the nature of cities, and the reuse of these voids can point us toward new opportunities and solutions.

0755 Garden of Ghosts, a private garden in Glebe, Sydney, Australia, is an example of landscapes that are slow and require patience and commitment to develop.

0756 A less structured version of a formal rose patch is the cottage rose garden. It usually has irregular shapes and a mix of perennial shrubs. Low-growing plants, such as carpet roses, mixed with climbing roses, such as the white iceberg rose to add height, will create the base of the garden and help you decide where to plant any surrounding plants.

0757 The Red Sand Garden is the central feature of the Australian Garden designed by Taylor Cullity Lethlean. Its vibrant red sand, crescent-shaped dunes and seasonal blooms of wildflowers remind one of the shapes and colors found in Central Australia.

Site plan

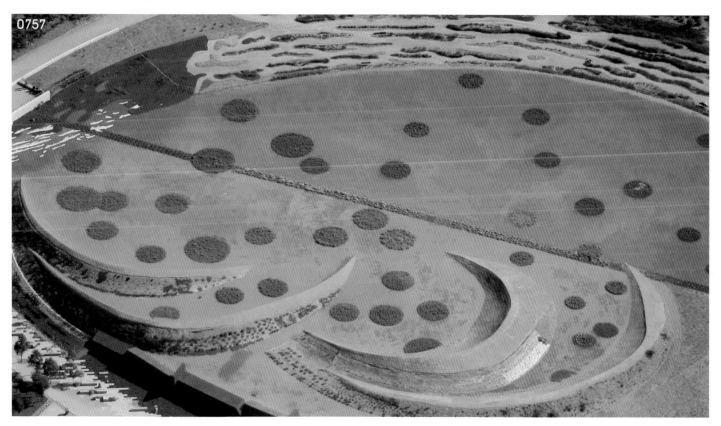

0758 In a formal garden design, low planting should be near the house, marking paths and axes. Trees should be planted away from the house to accommodate the particular rooting habits and to avoid conflict with underground utilities.

0759 Plants provide beauty and privacy around a pool, but there are some considerations that need to be taken into account when selecting the species, such as leaf litter falling into the pool and vigorous roots that can damage the pool.

0760 Herbs can be tucked among other plant species in beds and borders. One important thing to keep in mind is that herbs can be rampant plants and many spread by seed and by runners.

0761 Wild garden plants with bright colors and large leaves should be placed in the foreground so their details can be better appreciated. Those with small leaves and flowers should be kept at the back.

0762 The formal French garden is above all a design made to impress. Flowers are generally secondary in this type of design and can be restricted to a limited selection of bedding plants surrounded by low-clipped hedges.

Artist's impression

0763

0764

0765

0763 Beds and borders, and additional features such as ponds and fountains, make first-class focal points in paved gardens and allow you to avoid the inconvenience of maintaining large planted areas.

0764 In addition to size and shape, take into account the colors of your plant selections. The plants should go with their surroundings. Pebbles or boulders can be used to add texture and can contribute to an easy gardening philosophy.

0765 The composition and an appropriate selection of plants are what count in a minimal design, which relies on a visually aesthetic use of hard landscaping elements mixed with a few well-selected plants.

0766 Planters can be made in a variety of materials, shapes, widths and depths. They can be an effective way to mark circulation paths without having to resort to an extensive excavation project.

0767 Beyond their ornamental function, the shape and disposition of planting beds can help reinforce the architecture and integrate it into the site. The design of the exterior of a building should not be an afterthought but an integral part of the overall design composition.

0768 Sheared evergreen shrubs are preferred over deciduous specimens because they look good all year round. The ideal plants for shearing are boxwood, holly, yew, privet, pycarantha, box honeysuckle, thuja, junipers, and hemlocks.

0769 A free-form planting bed with a rich variety of plants combined with rocks of different sizes can be an interesting counterpoint to an immaculately mowed lawn.

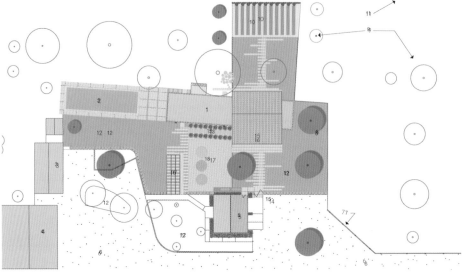

1. House
2. Pool
3. Existing guest house
4. Existing shop
5. Existing garage
6. Driveway
7. Existing fence
8. New trees
9. Existing trees
10. Vegetable garden
11. Existing walnut garden
12. Lawn
13. Herb garden
14. Gate
15. Shade and shelter canopy
16. Arbor
17. Flowers

Site plan

0770

0771

0770 Various planters of different sizes organize the design of the courtyard and delimit the paths, while the color and the shape of the diverse species of succulents and grasses are used to create patterns.

0771 The design concept of this plot is inspired by the traditional Japanese garden, while the selection of plant species is based on the availability in the region.

0772 Meticulous pruning transforms the landscape, changing the topography in shape and color. It can create focal points, define the perimeter of an area, and provide a privacy screen.

0773 The footprint of a long and narrow terrace is made more interesting by means of planting boxes to match the wood deck. The design is completed with a selection of tall grasses that provide privacy and create pleasant rustling sounds.

0774 Tall shrubs and trees enclose a space and lead the eye to a focal point. Plants can be arranged and combined in an infinite variety to bring about balance, unity and rhythm.

0775 Perfectly maintained ground cover with groups of trees contained within rings of grasses next to a lagoon make the perfect setting for a quiet retreat.

0776 A modular grid is formed by a pergola structure that organizes the space. Whatever occurs in each module, the overall grid is unified by a rhythmic repetition of the modules across the site.

0777 Sand and rocks are integral to traditional Japanese gardens. Sand in Japanese gardens represents a large expanse (the sea) that is filled with objects (the islands). When it is raked, it symbolizes gentle waves.

0778 Low-voltage lighting can round off a landscape composition by highlighting specific plant specimens and bringing out textures. Fixtures generally come in colors that blend well with foliage, but fixtures with higher visibility are available to complement your home's exterior design.

0779 Different plant supports, such as pots, planter boxes and the ground, make for a more interesting garden structure. It especially works in roof gardens, where the minimum soil depth needed may be limited by the load-bearing strength of the roof structure.

0780 A narrow passage is made visually interesting by placing several trees in planting boxes made of salvaged wood. The row of boxes adds rhythm without minimizing the perspective effect.

0781 Planters can add interest to a garden whether they sit on the ground or hang. Old farming tools can make interesting containers for your plants.

0782 Various species of plants are used on the different levels, creating platforms where texture, size and color play a big role. The use of plants in this confined space softens borders and edges without making the structure look cramped.

0783 Trellises and pergolas for climbing plants provide privacy and a detoxifying atmosphere. They create an ambiance and charm that are well worth the time and investment.

0784 Wood decks on a bed of gravel can be used to distinguish different zones. Gravel drains well, doesn't form puddles and is good for potted plants, as it aerates excessively compacted soil.

0785 In addition to its aesthetic character, a green roof, like the one shown here made of gravel and succulent plants, helps reduce the temperature of the building's interior. The plants used should be resistant to extreme weather conditions including heat, freezing and drought.

0786 Since the roof receives 100% of the sunlight, the plants selected should be able to withstand direct sun and wind. The presence of vegetation is crucial in cities since they help mitigate the effects of pollution absorbing CO_2 and emitting O_2.

0787 Green roofs retain much of the rain that falls on them, and maintaining proper drainage is very important. Parapets, edges, flashing, skylights, mechanical systems, vents, and chimneys must be well protected with a gravel skirt and sometimes a weeping drain pipe.

0782

0783

0784

0785

0786

0787

0788 Depth should be considered when determining whether the plants will stabilize in 10 or 24 inches (25 or 63 cm) of growing medium. It is crucial to know where the plants have been growing and if the growing conditions are comparable to a roof.

0789 Grasses, mosses, sedums, sempervivums, festuca, irises and wildflowers are typically employed in the design of extensive green roofs. In contrast to the unlimited selection of plants that can be found in intensive green roofs, these plants are native to dry lands.

0790 A variety of green roof systems can be created: from low-maintenance sedum matting and wildflower meadows to landscaped roof gardens with lawns, shrubs and small trees.

0791 Ground cover plants with attractive foliage can be a good addition to embellish and add tranquility to the stillness of your pond. The species that produce rhizomes or spread by offsets make great lawns.

0792 Decorative aggregates are ideal for adding natural features to your garden. Not only do they enhance the look of your garden, they also have practical and environmental advantages: during the growing season they can prevent unwanted weeds and slugs.

0793

0794

0795

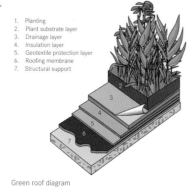

1. Planting
2. Plant substrate layer
3. Drainage layer
4. Insulation layer
5. Geotextile protection layer
6. Roofing membrane
7. Structural support

Green roof diagram

0793 Living Pavilion, designed by Behin + Ha, employs milk crates as the framework for a planting system similar to that of a green wall. Its surface is planted with shade-tolerant plants that create a cool environment thanks to the evapotranspiration from the plants.

0794 This garden covers the ventilation stack on the roof of a supermarket located below the interior courtyard of a housing block. The garden is the result of the neighbors' request to improve the landscape of the courtyard.

0795 Waterproofing systems for vertical gardens tend to be simpler than those for flat green roofs, as the stagnation of water has less potential to cause a problem. Nevertheless, the success of the system is dependent upon the quality of the installation.

0796 The main element at Erie Street Plaza, in Milwaukee, Wisconsin, by Stoss Landscape urbanism is a hybridized plaza-green with pavers and lawn surfaces that allow for both intense activity and more passive uses. The plaza is articulated as an eroded field of custom pre-cast pavers distributed to maximize variability and flexibility.

0797 Abundant vegetation is beneficial to the living environment as it helps cool off the interior spaces thanks to the evapotranspirations of plants.

0798 The Living Pavilion by Ann Ha and Behrang Behin is a temporary structure made of reclaimed milk crates on which plants are grown. It was built on Governor's Island, New York, and provides refuge from the heat by keeping the sheltered space cool by the evaporation from its planted surface.

0796

0797

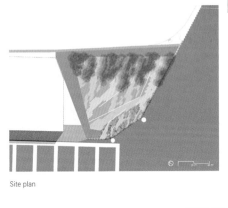
Site plan

0798

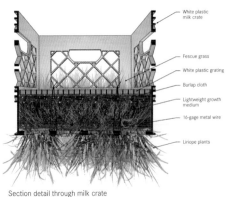
White plastic milk crate
Fescue grass
White plastic grating
Burlap cloth
Lightweight growth medium
16-gage metal wire
Liriope plants

Section detail through milk crate

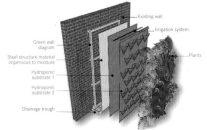
0799

0800

Green wall diagram

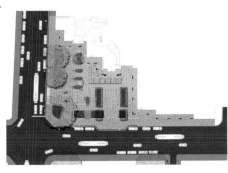
Site plan

0799 The vegetation has an ornamental function and serves to enhance the strong architectural quality of the square and, at the same time, to soften the rigidity of the stone.

0800 A green wall serves as a thermal and acoustic insulator and cleanses the air but does not have structural properties. It consists of a construction that incorporates a hydroponic system with a controlled irrigation system.

0801 The house is sheltered by the abundant vegetation. Boora Architects designed this house in response to the client's desire for a home offering simplicity, order and peace.

0801

0802

0803

0804

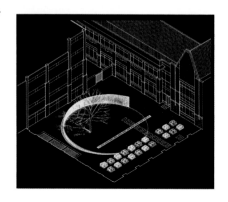

0805

0806

0807

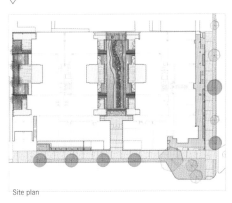

Site plan

Hand-drawn section through garden

0802 Taketo Shimohigoshi introduced a green element to contrast with the stark concrete residential building located at the edge of a commercial district in Tokyo, Japan. The building features a series of beams planted with hydroponically grown moss.

0803 The floral design of this courtyard is meant to be enjoyed from the building's higher windows. At the courtyard's level, the design may be difficult to appreciate and may only be perceived as organic shapes.

0804 Located on the Medtronic premises in Fridley, near Minneapolis, Minnesota, this garden is characterized by pure formal clarity and Zen inspiration.

0805 This apartment building courtyard makes a strong pictorial statement that can be enjoyed from the apartments' balconies. The design commemorates the 50th anniversary of the discovery of the DNA structure.

0806 The São Vicente's Caves Park is part of the Volcano Center complex. The site is arranged in terraces and integrates large landscaped areas around the pre-existing elements.

0807 A formal garden made of hedges and grasses is contained by existing woods. Within the garden, several groups of trees may serve as landmarks.

0808 ASPECT Studios designed a courtyard for a residential building in Bondi, Australia, just a block away from the ocean. The courtyard is the focus of the building and is meant to be viewed but not entered. It sits atop a platform, and its design is based on the layers carved by the wash of the surf on the shoreline.

0809 This partially covered garden in Victoria, Australia, designed by Taylor Cullity Lethlean, is presented as a densely populated patch of trees, where paths take visitors through various thematic areas representing the causes behind changes in the forest: water, earth, climate, man and fire.

0810 Anchor Park in Malmö, Sweden, was conceived by SLA as a new type of park: a "hydroglyph park." An open space by the water invites a contemplative pause. It incorporates elements of the natural surroundings of the area, such as alder marshes and oak woods, as well as the salt-water biotopes with crayfish.

0811 The Riekerpolder Plaza around the new IBM office building is part of the urban development plan in the south side of Amsterdam, the Netherlands. Delta Vorm Groep designed a natural environment marked by water, where a long and narrow pool in a central terrace that serves as a meeting point spills down into a larger pond through a water ladder.

0812 The concrete water channel defines the edges of the pavement types and delineates the pedestrian paths. Its simple design created by GTL Gnüchtel Triebswetter contrasts with the exuberant vegetation that surrounds Saint Bonifatius Hospital in Lingen, Germany.

0813 The Maanplein in the Hague is a well-balanced combination of architecture, infrastructure and landscape. The layout of the park, by Delta Vorm Groep, magnifies the strong volumetric value of the building complex and is reinforced by the reflecting pool, which adds dimension to the garden experience.

0814 GTL Gnüchtel Triebswetter included a low canalized water course in the design for Saint Bonifatius Hospital's surroundings in Lingen, Germany. The water spills over the ledge of one side and into a trough along the sidewalk, creating visual interest and a pleasant sound.

0815 The renovation of a garden center in Hamburg, Germany, was carried out by Glaser und Dagenbach following a minimalist approach that integrates elements from the French garden style. The design is organized around a black granite pond and white marble fountain.

Site plan

0814

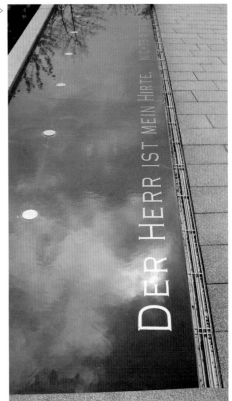

DER HERR IST MEIN HIRTE.

0815

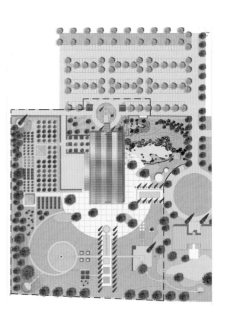

Site plan

0816

0817

0818

0819

0816 The grounds of the Walden Studios in the flood plain of the Russian River in California were converted by Andrea Cochran into a setting that draws on the memory of the site's agricultural past. The landscape is punctuated by fruit tree orchards that fuse with the natural surroundings in the image reflected in the mirror pool.

0817 The waterscape designs of Atelier Dreiseitl, such as Fornebu Park in Oslo, Norway, address the fields of urban hydrology, storm water management, urban planning and landscape architecture. The large blocks of stone placed randomly on the pavement flooded by a thin sheet of water call to mind gigantic icebergs grinding against the shallows.

0818 oslund.and.assoc. created a functional outdoor workshop for the Laboratory Science Building of the University of Minnesota, Duluth. An experimental pond is divided by a concrete weir. The lower half of the pond receives the storm water runoff, while the upper half is a water garden that emphasizes the cultivation of wild rice.

0819 Within the limits of a large park in Stuttgard, Germany, Michael Singer designed a garden where two small streams converge and are augmented by three wells. The water collects in pools that reveal shapes below their surface and planters made of granite, precast concrete and bronze.

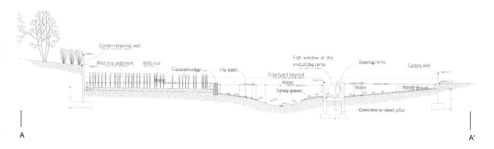

A
A'

Pond section

0820 Solar City is a large residential complex in Linz, Austria. The design of the open spaces in and around this development is aimed to control the anticipated high user pressure that could be exerted on the sensitive alluvial forests along the Traun River.

0821 The office of Vetsch Nipkow Partner Landschaftsarchitekten was commissioned for the rejuvenation of the open spaces around a former factory complex in Winterthur, Switzerland. The result is a series of dynamic spaces where the pavement is in some parts recessed to collect rain water, becoming temporary reflecting pools.

0822 For the expansion of the General Mills Corporate Campus in Minnesota, the landscape architecture office of oslund.and.assoc. conceived a setting that creates the illusion that the new buildings are floating on a motionless plane of water.

0823 West 8 designed Chiswick Park in collaboration with Richard Rogers Partnership within a new office district in central London, England. The park makes reference to 19th-century Chinese paintings with water lily ponds, a timber boardwalk, rocks and grasses.

Computer-generated rendering of the park

0824 Landscape architects TROP proposed a series of pools for a narrow courtyard between two long residential buildings in Hua Hin, Thailand's popular beach resort. Due to the configuration of the development, not all the apartments enjoy the views of the sea. Instead, they enjoy a pleasant seascape of pools, garden islands and boulders.

0825 The inner courtyards of the T-Mobile City in Bonn, Germany, are conceived based on the idea of water surfaces mirroring the facades of the buildings. Stephan Lenzen Landschaftsarchitekten created circular islands with vegetation that can be accessed via stepping stones.

0826 Water is an integral element in Australian Garden, designed by the landscape architecture office of McGregor Coxall. James Turrell's Within Without monolithic work appears to be sunken in a large pond surrounded by lawn terraces.

0827 The "water square" is a thematic staging of the unique river landscape of Burghausen, Germany, on the occasion of a state garden show. Within a stony area, the water level constantly rises and falls, symbolizing the periods of drought and flood that affect the Salzach River. Above water level, wooden decks emphasize the natural process.

0828 The pool at the Hilton Central Pattaya Hotel in Thailand forms a soothing bath, thanks to its curvilinear shape. The landscape architecture office of TROP cleverly sectioned the pool below the water surface into nooks with bubbly hot tubs. Randomly placed planters with mangroves bring nature to a highly sophisticated hotel decoration.

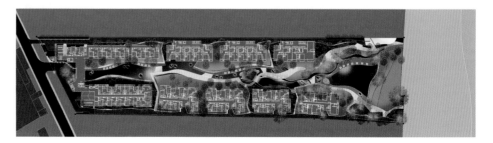

Development site plan with 755-ft. (230 m) long pool courtyard

0829 TROP designed the roof terrace of a luxury condominium tower in Bangkok, Thailand with lush vegetation and comfortable day beds aligning a long infinity pool overlooking the city's skyline.

0830 The elegant lobby of the Hilton Central Pattaya Hotel in Thailand is open to a shallow pool. TROP designed a sculptural fence and included lush plants to complete an exotic arrival experience that inspires maximum comfort in peaceful, natural surroundings.

0831 TROP's combination of high-quality craftsmanship and careful material selection responds to their clients' high level requirements. This image illustrates a variety of edge conditions, such as stepped, cantilever or planting.

0832 The concept of an infinity pool or vanishing-edge pool seems to have been inspired by the effect of the terraced rice paddies of Indonesia. In this image, the illusion of its edge extending to the horizon forms the perfect synergy between the body of water and its architectural surroundings.

0833 Infinity pools require a trough to collect the water flowing over the submerged edge and a pump that recirculates the water back into the pool. In the appropriate setting, the results can be spectacular.

0834 The polygonal shapes of the two pools echo the steel posts and fiberglass canopies, which were inspired by the pine trees that dominate the natural landscape of the Spanish coastal town of Vila-Seca, near Tarragona.

0835 In this modern residence, the position and orientation of the pool were two of the factors that determined its shape. Two large geometric porticos define the space like picture frames acting as a threshold, inviting the viewer to contemplate the garden beyond.

0836 Making the most of the existing natural environment by integrating it into the landscape concept whenever possible preserves the authentic appearance of the landscape with minimal input, as in this image, where a pool embraces the existing rock formation.

0837 Water in its many forms animates both soft and hard landscapes, such as these water features in the HM Treasury courtyards in London, England, by the landscape architecture office Gustafson Porter.

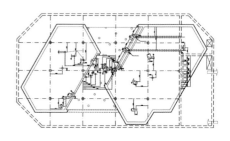

Pool plan for Pinar dels Perruquets urban park by Arteks Arquitectura in Vila-Seca, Spain

0838

0838 Water elements add movement to the park landscape and act as an audible relaxant. By creating stages within the system for water to flow through, Cyprus architects Ioakim-Loizas begin telling a story which in turn guides the user.

0839 Ioakim-Loizas designed this pool to define the space around it, taking into account the circulation and use of the space. In a pool, even more so than in any other public space, the human body interacts with the materials. Therefore it is imperative to consider the qualities and combination of the finishes, colors, and level changes.

0840 Infinity pools have become an incomparable water feature whose strategic disposition achieves the idyllic fusion of all the landscape features around it and communicates a seamless visual continuity toward the surroundings.

0841 This project reproduces the famous natural flooding of Piazza San Marco in Venice, Italy. This project reuses a former warehouse located under the banks of the Garonne River in Toulouse, France, that now houses the mechanical system that allows the artificial flooding of the 29,000 sq. feet (2,694 m²) square.

0839

0840

0841

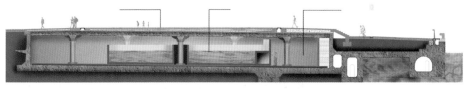

Section through water and reservoir

0842

0843

0844

0845

0842 An interior courtyard with a pool is the way architect Jos van de Lindeloof chose to green up the work environment of this office building.

0843 On the seventh floor of a 42-story residential tower in Hong Kong and built on top of a parking garage, the striking shape of a pool takes center stage, creating a bold spatial statement while organizing the various spaces around it.

0844 A sense of entry is achieved by a courtyard with a reflecting pool set in a bed of slate chippings. The white and gray Zen-like setting is animated by the Japanese koi carps agitating the water.

0845 Borders, transitions, changes in level, sound and reflection provide spatial quality and distinction to a site. This design of the Sawa office park, in Zoetermer, the Netherlands, by Rijnboutt, takes full advantage of the qualities that water has to offer to create a memorable space.

0846 SWA planned the Westlake Corporate Campus, west of Dallas, Texas, integrating the architecture with the natural surroundings of forests, meadows and ponds. Sandstone is the predominant material used to build the office building and the watercourses, which handle the site drainage while providing a useful amenity.

0847 Las Margas Parks and Public Gardens by Verzone Woods Architectes is a series of new lakes, public promenades and parks that play an important role in connecting a nearby residential neighborhood to the abundant number of outdoor activities that already exist in the Tena Valley, Spain.

0848 Extravagant gardens with topiaries and decorative statues arranged around large pools are images that come to our mind when we think of elegant Italian Renaissance villas. In fact, it was during this period that Italians developed their own style of gardening and architecture for waterways.

0849 Users of this pool surely must appreciate the privacy of a tall stone wall on one side while enjoying the view of the landscape on the opposite side.

0850 A small pond is turned into a central feature of a rooftop garden. Wooden Planters at all four corners and benches of the same material surrounding the pond make the most for a moment of reflection in a Zen-like surrounding.

0851 The cantilever deck extends over the edge of the pool, offering a modern look. However, a cantilever coping is more difficult to install than a traditional bull nose coping.

0852 A skewed pool in a formal gravel and hedge garden adds dynamism and an additional layer of complexity to the otherwise static and bland garden surrounded by tall walls and dense vegetation.

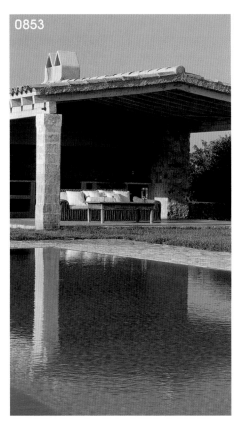

0853

0853 The flagstone pavement of this rural property was carefully cut to insert an infinity pool. Natural stones cut in irregular shapes create texture and warmth around an in ground pool.

0854 While the roof's load-bearing strength must be taken into consideration before installing a pool, the structure should be plenty strong to hold a hot tub and turn the otherwise dismal roof terrace into an oasis.

0855 Nested among pine trees on a rocky costal hillside with views of the sea, this is the ultimate luxury retreat complete with a hot tub overlooking the pools.

0854

0855

0856 Water is essential to Moroccan-style courtyards. Water features in this style not only bring the cool effect of water, but they also add a vibrant splash of color.

0857 The interface between the old and the new provides all kinds of technical challenges that are worth exploring in accordance with the setting. Masonry ruins, especially rubble stonework, will add romantic appeal to a pool garden.

0858 The technical aspect of water recirculation is explored and used as a visual asset, made of a narrow channel of water around the pool and a spout at one end of it.

0859 The stand-out feature of this luxury property with far-reaching views is a stunning infinity pool that seems to flow into the woods.

0860

0861

0862

0863

0860 A channel for the recirculated pool water forms a ring around a section of the lawn, planted with trees. The channel then spouts down into a lower basin.

0861 At the dip between two low knolls, a stone wall frames the long pool at one end, and water spouts from the top of the wall to drizzle down the front into the pool.

0862 The design of this pool successfully addresses the philosophical challenge of how to modify an existing structure. The salvaged stones of an old farm have been used to build a pool in the middle of vineyards and olive orchards.

0863 An infinity pool integrates best in the natural landscape. The irregular shape on three sides and a few rocks immersed in the pool are best for a greater effect.

0864 Create a spectacular outdoor room as a spot for relaxation with a hot tub and pool that suits your needs and defines your style. Also, think of this investment as a way to increase the value of your home.

0865 The design of this property in Ocotal Beach, Costa Rica, includes an overflow pool that surrounds the house, giving it the impression of a floating home.

0866 Infinity pools don't seem out of place in a natural setting. On the contrary, a simple wall made of local stone helps integrate the pool into the natural surroundings.

0867 This is another creative example of how to incorporate a water recirculation channel into the design of an infinity pool, here contained by stone walls in a grass field.

0868

0868 An interior space is opened to a pool and to the views beyond. A sheet of water pours from above the ceiling to cool the interior space without having to resort to air conditioning.

0869 At dusk and accompanied by the views of the distant hills, submerged lighting adds a softening glow to the pool area, making the poolside an elegant lounge space.

0870 Reflected in the water surface, the structure of the pergola seems to extend below the surface of the water.

0869

0870

0871

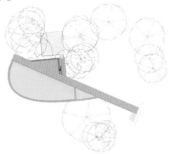

Site plan

0871 Set at the edge of a steep hill, hugging the edge of the knoll where it sits, the pool follows the contoured lines of the site.

0872 At night, the lights reveal the materials used in the pool and the detail of the vegetation around it. When choosing lights for your pool, take into account that there are different types of lights depending on the material the walls of the pool are made of and, therefore, different installation methods.

0873 While we may be accustomed to seeing a water recirculation trough a few inches below the spilling edge of the pool, this is a creative alternative and an example of the innumerable possibilities to approach the technical requirement.

0874 In the twilight, the edge of the pool is barely perceptible, making the pool part of the sea in the horizon and a mirrored surface that captures the changes of colors of the surrounding landscape.

0872

0873

0874

0875

0875 The design of a trough in which the pool water spills can go beyond its functional character. It can become a pleasant running water feature that contrasts with the stillness of the pool surface.

0876 Organically shaped pools give the illusion of being part of nature, and most importantly, they are free-form and can adapt to the constraints of a small site. Limited only by imagination, they are even more striking when illuminated.

0876

0877 With natural landscaping tying together lush elements with the efficient use of space, a rock pool can provide a site without character with a resort feeling.

0878 The pool incorporates little islets of rocks and plants. The composition is a scale representation of a real body of water with islands.

0879 Beyond its utilitarian function, the trough below the spilling level of the pool acquires its own identity, giving the impression of a lower pool onto which an upper one sits.

0880 Rather than an isolated element, this pool is integrated into the structure of the house, whose ground floor extends to become a terrace then folds to create the shape of the pool.

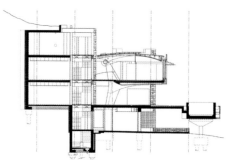

Section through house and pool

0881 Infinity pools must be built to precise standards and regulations with a perfectly level edge to be effective. While these rules are strict and must be complied with for public use, they might be more flexible in the context of a home.

0882 Outdoor pools act like liquid canvases that depict the surroundings. Since the water is rarely still, the image reflected on the water surface dances and shines in the sunlight.

0883 In this image, the design of this pool harmonizes the size, the shape and the geometry of the architecture and the surrounding landscape. In general, a pool provides a focal point.

0884 The site was built up and flattened to accommodate the pool. Because it is positioned on the crest of a hill, the horizontal plane of water seems to float in the view.

0885 Vo Trong Nghia Co designed the Bamboo Wing, an open public space in the middle of a park in Hanoi, Vietnam, that seems to emerge from a large pool. This design is aimed to take advantage of the cooling effect of the water.

0886 To comply with safety regulations, the stair nosing comes in a non-slip abrasive finish and is usually rounded. It is also tiled in a different color from the rest of the stair.

0887 This café is surrounded by artificial lakes that at first glance, give the impression of being very deep, but it is the black stone and the curved bottom of the lake that give the illusion of greater depth.

0888 The wNw bar is located in an artificial lake. It uses natural wind energy and the cool water from the lake to create natural air ventilation. A 5-foot (1.5 m) diameter opening at the peak of the roof allows for the evacuation of the hot air that accumulates inside.

0889 The maintenance of natural pools is minimal since they require no chemical treatment and the natural purification of the water takes place near the swimming area. This system mimics the behavior of purifying microorganisms in natural bodies of water.

0890 A cooling effect is achieved through evaporation. This house is surrounded by two ponds that cool off the sections that are closest to them using this method. In the winter, the water accumulates heat and diffuses it into the high thermal inertia walls of the house.

0891 In the spring and fall, maintenance of natural pools in good conditions does not require much effort. In the summer, natural pools must be taken care of at least once a week.

0892 The catalyst for this unconventional pool pavilion in the Napa Valley, California, was a "sky space" by artist James Turrell, which is located in a swimming pool and can be entered by swimming underwater.

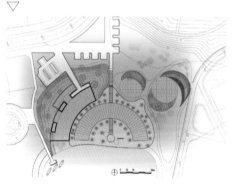

Site plan

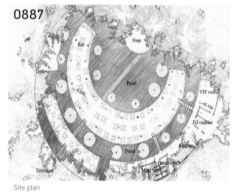

Site plan

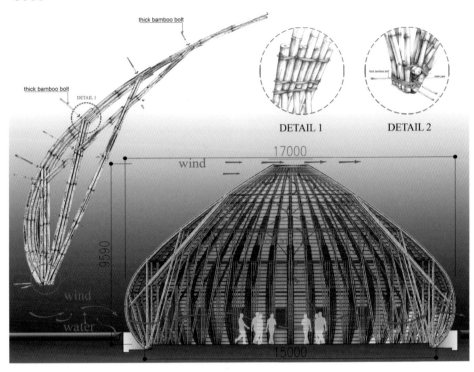

thick bamboo bolt

thick bamboo bolt

DETAIL 1

DETAIL 1

DETAIL 2

17000

wind

9590

wind

water

15000

Diagram of the natural ventilation system

0889

0890

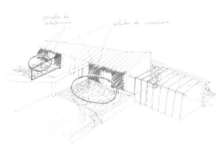

Diagram of the cooling and heating system through evaporation of water

0891

0892

0893 The design for this pool pavilion in Napa Valley, California, designed by Tom Leader Studio, involved re-organizing the entire topography.

0894 Lighting enhances the shape of the pool and transforms it into a focal point of the terrace. Because of its organic shape, it helps integrate the rest of the architecture into the site.

0895 The wavy shape of the pool mimics the movement of the waves of the sea below, and the selection of the materials evokes the sandy beach and crystalline turquoise waters.

0896 A T-shape pool marks two axes that connect different areas of the property. At the same time, it allows for lap swimming and playing without one interfering with the other.

0897 With rising environmental awareness, more and more home owners want a pool that relies on biological water treatment and, therefore, is in harmony with nature.

0898 Surrounded on two sides by the pool, the house appears to be built on top of the water surface, giving a floating effect. The light appearance of the house reinforces this effect.

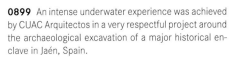

0899 An intense underwater experience was achieved by CUAC Arquitectos in a very respectful project around the archaeological excavation of a major historical enclave in Jaén, Spain.

0900 Palmyra House, located outside Mumbai, India, was designed by Studio Mumbai. A central pool in a plaza between two louvered structures connects the views of the sea to the west and the views into the dense forest to the east. Locally quarried black basalt was used to construct the stone plinths and the pool.

0901 The use of biological treatment for swimming pool water is increasing, especially when designing a new pool. In biological treatments, microorganisms are used to decompose organic matter.

0902 The design of this pool is an example of an effective fusion between architecture and landscape. A colorful selection of plants completes the area forming a screen of vegetation.

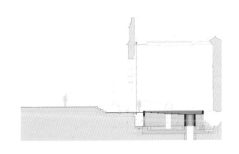

Section through historic enclave and renovation

0903

0904

0905

Site plan

0906

0907

0903 In the context of De Nieuwe Ooster Cemetery in Amsterdam, the Netherlands, Karres en Brands explores special forms of burial such as a long strip of water that holds cinerary urns.

0904 A water park in Bucaramanga, Colombia, is a public space where water determines the character of the walkways and of the different areas within the park in the form of fountains, waterfalls, jets, trickles and ponds.

0905 This pool is a salvaged water tank with its surface flush with the terrace. Lundberg Design used recycled materials for the construction of this home to better integrate it into the natural environment.

0906 In biologically treated pools, there is first a pump-operated water circuit at the surface of the water with a mechanical filter device. There is a second pump-operated water circuit with a biological filter and an anion exchanger arranged downstream of the latter. This system allows the purification of the water without the use of toxic disinfectants.

0907 There is nothing more captivating than being in a room with its foundations in a body of water. With all sides open and feeling the breeze, one could imagine being in a luxury resort on a Polynesian beach.

0908 The trees in the garden and the stone of the wall that protects the pool create an attractive, simple space. A row of vertical stone blocks act as sculptures that create a play of shadows and reflections on the pool surface.

0909 In what we call "natural ponds," the water treatment takes place by means of water plants and biological filters and does not require chlorine or other toxic chemicals.

0910 Slightly elevated from the ground, the pool occupies a predominant place in this garden, which invites relaxation but can also be the setting for elegant soirées.

0911 Solbjerg Square is an urban space of dark natural stone milled with small circular recesses that fill with water when it rains, transforming the continuous plane into a vibrant water landscape of reflecting pools. The water experience is enhanced by gratings set in the pavement spewing clouds of mist.

0912 Janet Rosenberg + Associates designed an active entrance courtyard for the historic Mackenzie building in downtown Toronto, Canada. The courtyard, which includes two recuperated ginkgo trees and a simple water feature, is visible from the street and has become an important part of Toronto's downtown experience.

0913 Noerresundby Urban Garden in Aalborg, Denmark, designed by SLA, is formed by a series of platforms on top of a graveled area. The platforms create shallow pools with jets that engage children, especially in recreational activities.

0914

0914 The Fountain Promenade, designed by Grupo de Diseño Urbano (GDU) in Mexico City, Mexico, is part of Chapultepec Park. The promenade is marked by a reflecting pool punctuated by various water features and bridges to engage visitors.

0915 The surroundings of the IBM headquarters in Amsterdam, the Netherlands, are a large expanse of lawn with a series of interconnected pools that serve to connect the different parts of the complex.

0916 The landscaping of the open spaces among office buildings in the Hague, the Netherlands emphasizes the presence of the park as a continuous body that flows among the different volumes, imitating incidental forms found in nature and contrasting with the orthogonal character of the architecture.

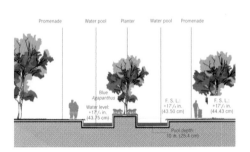

0915

0916

0917 A series of reinforced fiberglass concave forms are fountains located in the square at the base of the Infineon Asia Pacific Headquarters designed by GTL Gnüchtel Triebswetter Landschaftsarchitekten in Singapore.

0918 A square in Aalborg, Denmark, integrates circular stepped fountains that remind one of rings of water. In summertime they are used to cool off and play, and in wintertime they are playful sculptures for climbing.

0919 The surroundings of Saint Bonifatius Hospital in Lingen, Germany, designed by GTL Gnüchtel Triebswetter Landschaftsarchitekten, include a large planted area and a space for outdoor seating with fountains imbedded in a long stone low wall.

0920 For the redevelopment of one of the areas close to the waterfront of the city of Fredericia in Denmark, Birk Nielsen created a striking promenade with jigsaw elements that protrude from the granite pavement. These elements establish a dialog with the tall water jets.

0921 The design of a stepped fountain creates an invigorating entry focal point. Meticulous attention is paid to details to achieve the effect of falling water combined with the glistening texture of the different colors of granite in the sunlight.

0922 So simple and yet the result is dramatic. The design of the spill edge produces a clear, rib-free flow into the awaiting pool.

0923 Water sprayed from a jet or spewed from a spigot tends to follow a parabolic path. The particular arc is determined by the angle of the jet and the speed at which water leaves the jet.

0924 The shape and the texture of a channel affect the flow of the water. A rough and shallow channel offers a considerable amount of friction, resulting in slow flow.

0925 Graceful parabolic streams of water can offer lessons in geometric spectacle. The shape of the nozzle is very important to achieve the desired effect. In most cases, the jets become wider and fuzzier as they shoot farther out.

0926 Atelier Dreiseitl created an open public space with stepping stones and small wavy wedges to produce interesting flow patterns over shallow canals.

0927 For the redevelopment of the city center of Barleben, Germany, Atelier Dreiseitl created a striking streetscape. The special highlights of this renovation are the light and water sculptures which, day and night, mark the middle of town.

0928 The water flow created by the shape and texture of the water channel generates sculptural forms in movement that stimulate our visual and hearing senses.

0929 Landscape architect Arne Saelen was commissioned to design a roundabout in the city center of Vejle, Denmark. The roundabout is composed of two granite oval halves set apart and sinking to make room for a passage. Water cascades over the surfaces of the inclined blocks and flows under the passage.

0930 With Tanner Springs, Atelier Dreiseitl successfully recaptures the area's past with its native wetlands and flowing rills. The springs connect the park to Tanner Creek, which at one time flowed openly through this area.

0931 For the 2007 edition of the Bavarian garden exhibition in Waldkirchen, Germany, Rehwaldt Landaschaftsarchitekten designed various areas around the theme of water, such as an interactive touch table that controls the jets emerging from a nearby pool.

0932 One of the most striking features of the Australian Garden by Taylor Cullity Lethlean with Paul Thompson is the rock pool waterway and escarpment wall, an abstract representation of a natural setting with square blocks placed so that the visual effect and sound mimic those in nature.

Site plan

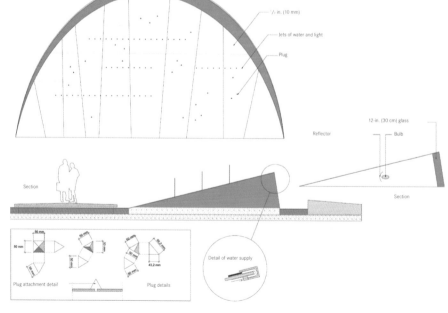

0930

0931

0932

0933 Toppilansaari Park in Oulu, Finland, is an area defined by two art gardens designed by Atelier Dreiseitl. For one of the gardens, Herbert Dreiseitl created a light "vortex," a sculpture made of recycled ship parts. The art piece sprays water and rotates like the lamp of a lighthouse.

0934 The waterfront of Tjuvholmen, a neighborhood of Oslo, Norway, has undergone a comprehensive transformation that includes three water features representing water's different states: a still pond in massive dark granite, a fountain with six jets and a third feature of rippling water inside a hollow rhombus-shaped porphyry pillar.

0935 The space below the north wing of Brockman Hall at Rice University in Houston, Texas, is a court dominated by a fountain that provides both a cooling effect and a reflecting surface to allow natural light to play off of the underside of the building.

0936 At the square of T-Mobile City, designed by RMP Stephan Lenzen Landschaftsarchitekten, water is a conductor, reflector and diffuser of light and color.

0937 Nansen Park in Oslo, Norway, by Bjørbekk & Lindheim, is on the site once occupied by the Oslo International Airport. The design of the water channel reflects the playful variations between straight and organic, still reflecting pool surfaces, streaming and falling water.

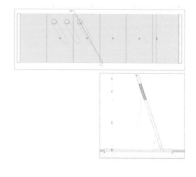

Water feature plan and section

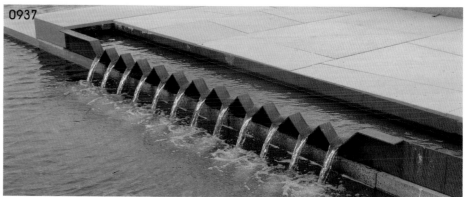

0938

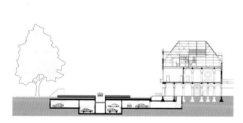

Section through pond on parking garage roof

0939

0940

0938 Bisected by the entrance of a car garage, an ornamental pond with a rim of Corten steel is part of the renovation of a block of luxury apartments in Heemstede, the Netherlands. At night, the light from the underground parking garage shines through shafts covered with colored glass, resulting in a special effect.

0939 Holmens Bruk is located along the Motala Stream in the city of Norrköping in Sweeden. Thorbjörn Andersson developed the site based on the landscape qualities of the stream and its banks as well as on the industrial heritage of the city.

0940 The office of James Burnett was commissioned to redevelop the Brochstein Pavilion's central courtyard at Rice University, Houston, Texas. Two black concrete fountains were placed in a grove of Allee lacebark elms, filling the garden with the murmur of running water and reflecting the filtered light through the trees.

0941

0942

0943

0944

0945

0941 Water Park was designed for Expo 2008 by aldayjover arquitectura y paisaje around the theme of water and sustainable development. Except for a bathing area, which is protected from the effects of the Ebro River annual flooding, the meander provides overflow space and natural filtering.

0942 For the Hilton Pattaya in Thailand, TROP designed a drop-off area at ground floor, level and the hotel garden on the 16th floor above a shopping mall. The arrival court sits on top of a shallow pool of black stone with small jets of water that keep the water moving.

0943 In 2004, Michael Singer and CH2MHill were selected to lead the re-imaging process and design for a cohesive West Palm Beach Waterfront Commons, Florida. The revitalization of the waterfront includes several unique water gardens that help reconnect the city with the sea.

0944 The new esplanade, part of the West Palm Beach Waterfront revitalization project, consists of several discreet spaces, including intimate seating areas and small event "rooms" along a continuous bike and pedestrian path, as well as a unique water feature seating bench.

0945 Customized water spouts, sheer descent waterfalls and wet edges combine with a particular choice of materials to ensure that each water feature is unique.

0946 The expansion project of the Montjuïc Fairgrounds 2 in Barcelona, Spain, was developed by Japanese architect Toyo Ito in collaboration with JML Consultants. It consisted of a complex of pavilions interconnected by courtyards where a series of water features were designed to reflect the geometry of the architectural complex.

0946

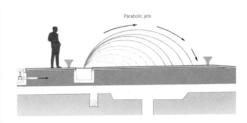

Parabolic jets

Section through water jet trough

0947

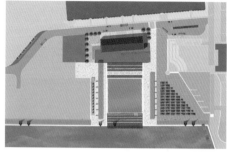

Site plan

0947 When the terminals for maritime traffic were moved outside of London, the Royal Walls situated on the shores of the Thames River suffered a period of decay. EDAW was in charge of designing a large square next to the East London Exhibition Center. The path to the ExCeL building is lined with fountains that confer solemnity to the entrance.

0948 In order to mitigate the traffic noise from the bustling city of Oslo, Norway, Bjørbekk & Lindheim made a water curtain in a restored pond in Pilestredet Park. The water curtain also brings some cooling effect to the park and has become a popular playful element.

0949 The remodeling of Čufarjev Square in the Slovenian city of Jesenice resulted in the creation of an open space capable of accommodating different types of events. The square is empty and the street fixtures are located at the edges. The multifunctional space is, however, integrated with water, a presence that is both visible and invisible.

0950 Bjørbekk & Lindheim integrated a small rill as a connecting feature through a new area with a kindergarten and sports facilities in Fornebu, Norway. At the same time, this element of running water offers recreational opportunities.

0948

0949

0950

0951 Čufar Square in the city center of Jesenice, Slovenia, incorporates water jets that propel water into the air in various combinations. Computer-controlled nozzles can be a good asset to attract visitors, hence turning the public space into a popular gathering space, especially at night.

0952 Rather than acting as an unconquerable barrier, the steep slope of the land may become an asset. Taking advantage of the topographical features, a rock garden was introduced instead of using retaining walls. At its feet, the rustic water cascade amid the tuft of pennisetum evokes a natural setting.

0953 Remember to exploit every bit of outdoor space, even the smallest one, which may turn into a landscaped haven. Implement a dry garden and work on the hardscape where no soil depth is applicable by using decorative pebbles and pots, trellised pergolas, water basins and wooden decks.

0954 Technologies and techniques developed in alternative fields can be used during the design process. Clay models were scanned using software from the automotive industry to generate 3-D computer files that were used to both design and cut the complex profiled stones for the Diana, Princess of Wales Memorial Fountain in London, England.

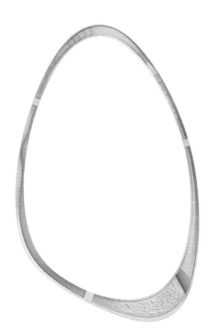

3-D computer-generated rendering of the Diana, Princess of Wales Memorial Fountain

0955 A water feature can be used as an architectural element. The high jet challenges the tall tower, creating a composition with two vertical signals that are visible from miles away.

0956 For Bercy Park in Paris, France, JML Consultants designed a grand stairway. Down its center is a water feature of cascading water. The sloping strips that canalize the water counterbalance the horizontality of the steps.

0957 Water has the power to reveal the quality of a nice detail but can also expose a construction fault. Designing with water is challenging, and attention to detail is critical to achieve the best effect.

0958 Water has an astonishing transformative capacity, and modern techniques allow designers to modify its state, artificially creating differences of pressure or temperature that transform water into solid or steam.

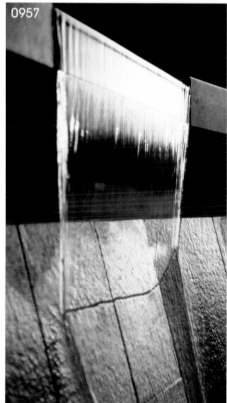

0959

0960

0961

0959 Sculptural elements can be a guiding influence in the garden experience and frame a focal point such as this water feature in the lake of a historic park in Delft, the Netherlands.

0960 Franklin Children's Garden, a park in Toronto's Center Island, Canada, was designed to teach children about natural ecosystems. Various elements in the park, such as this playful water feature, allow children to experience nature firsthand.

0961 The usual design of a spill edge is made to look like the water falls from one body of water into another. As the image shows, the forest in the background is made part of the composition.

0962 The Water Table Station Square in Apeldoorn, the Netherlands, is an example of how spaces can serve more than one purpose. It is a lively reflecting pond or a convenient stage for roller skating.

0962

0963 Atwater Place and the Ardea in Portland's South Waterfront, Oregon, combine a mixed-use high-rise residential district with retail and recreational facilities. Water was an integral element of the design and helped transform a former brown field into a dynamic public area.

0964 The Storaa Stream project by Okra has produced a series of public spaces in the cultural district in Holstebro, Denmark. With water as the design theme to reinforce the connection between the city and its river, Okra created an outdoor stage with a long water feature.

0965 The Enschede Market Square is a flexible space that emphasizes the constantly changing dynamics of its use. Series of elements can be added or taken out and moved from one position to another. On market days the square is bustling and on quiet days rows of misting nozzles create a completely different atmosphere.

0966 By using a pool punctuated with a large granite clad cube in the courtyard of a residential complex, a dramatic focal point has been created. The success of this design lies in the relationship of these two elements with their surroundings, notably its axial nature and the vertical echo of the proportions of the development.

0967 Projects are not isolated items and are part of a system of perceptual, functional and natural relations and processes. Care must be taken not to obstruct these relations, allowing their continuity and contribution to the environment.

0968 SWA developed a master plan for Chongqing's Tea Garden District, China; an active mixed-use development complete with community and neighborhood open spaces where water is a predominant element.

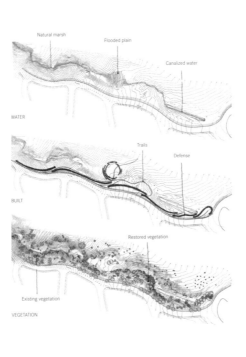

Site analysis diagrams

0969

0970

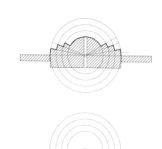

0971

0972

0969 The design for a square in Aalborg, Denmark, consists of granite water features to flood and outlet an ornamental lake. These sculptural features are designed as positive and negative forms, like ying and yang.

0970 A detail of the Wall of 100 Springs in a private courtyard in Little Bay, Sydney, Australia, shows us that detail is as important as the big picture. It invites us to rest, observe, admire and notice what is otherwise invisible. Beware: smallness makes even small mistakes appear important.

0971 A mist cloud at the Curtis Hixon Park riverfront plaza in Tampa, Florida, designed by Thomas Balsley, expresses the endless possibilities of water in the public landscape.

0972 A frog pond spitter is a classic way to accentuate a pond and add water movement. The spitter is usually fed by a submersible pond pump that circulates the water, helping aeration and providing flow to the biological filter.

0973 Bensley Design Studios has mastered the planning of high-end lifestyle resorts, spas and private residences so as not to detract from the natural surroundings.

0974 Bensley Design Studios is known for its designs of tropical gardens linked by open-air pathways. Working mostly in Asia, BDS's unconventional designs are sensual and hold special reverence for the tropical climate.

0975 With its refreshing approach to design, Bensley Design Studios reveals the artistry and aesthetics of traditional craftsmanship while creating contemporary structures that reinterpret old forms and materials in new and exciting ways.

0976 Water, rectilinear planes, brilliant colors and vegetation come together to form a serene environment. The vibrant blue color reinforces the effect of the water spouting out from the wall into a pool.

0977 Renaissance Italian-inspired gardens manifest themselves as peaceful retreats that highlight agriculture as much as ornamental plantings. They often include parterres, orchards, terraces, pergolas, patterned hardscapes, and water features that create focal points.

0978 Even the smallest yard is suitable for an appealing water feature. A vertical design occupies less usable space and is just as effective.

0979 A sleek black granite pond is the focus of this roof terrace. It contrasts with the wood-slated deck and with the old water tanks that characterize the skyline of New York.

0980 A nicely finished water feature combined with a fire pit is complemented with water lilies and grasses for a simple but attractive design.

0981 Using rock gardens or stone walls to grow alpines is a great way of replicating their natural habitat. Use topsoil or weed-free soil as your surface layer. Use protective material when placing your rocks into position. There should be enough for it to look like a realistic rocky setting but leave space for planting.

0982 A stepped water feature integrated into a pool brings soothing sounds. Made of textured concrete, it stands out in the rustic setting of natural stone and lush vegetation.

0980

0981

0982

0983 A play fountain has become the heart of the CityDeck, a redevelopment project by Stoss Landscape Urbanism along the Fox River in Green Bay, Wisconsin.

0984 The Pedestrian walkway of Deer Moat in Prague, Czech Republic, designed by AP Atelier, connects the Vltava River with a castle. The design of the pathway follows, for the most part, the route of the stream along the mountain.

0985 Since its origins in the 1930s, this water treatment plant provided the population with drinking water and with a recreational area until the 1990s, when the site was closed to the public. It was reopened in 2003 to be part, once again, of the public park system of the city.

0986 Water Park is the result of an effort carried out by the Bucaramanga Metropolitan Aqueduct Company, which hired Lorenzo Castro to convert a former water treatment plant in Bucaramanga, Colombia, into a public park. The renovation integrates the existing buildings, rescuing the historic character of the site.

0987

0988

0989

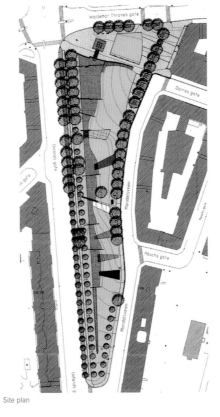

Site plan

0990

0987 The design of a public school's patio in Altdorf, Switzerland, consists of a graveled area that can accommodate different types of activities, from running and playing to large event meetings. The highlight of this simple composition and main attraction for children is a fountain, whose shape mimics the geometry of the area of the school.

0988 Massive mute limestone walls stand sentry over the pool. A simple composition of stone, water and grass is complemented by the play of light and shadow, and with the murmur of falling water.

0989 The Ila River, which flows 33 feet (10 m) underground through the city of Oslo, Norway, was brought to the surface and redirected through Alexander Kiellands Plass by way of a series of wells and water features using the natural slope of the land.

0990 The Roobeek River, which flows through Enschede, the Netherlands, gives its name to a commercial street. Flowing underground for a long time, it has been brought to the surface with a new redevelopment plan carried out by Buro Sant en Co. The stream flows around an original composition of stepping stones, taking inspiration from nature.

0991 Gaggiano is a medieval town on the Naviglio Grande canal, west of Milan, Italy. Its deteriorated shorelines inspired a restructuring project to restore the area as a pedestrian zone. Along with limestone and metal, water is introduced by way of fountains and springs.

0992 The need for storm water canalization can be an opportunity to bring an interesting landscape design element to the urban fabric, transforming this functional system into an aesthetic component of a streetscape.

0993 Harbor Square is an emblematic public space in the historic center of Thisted, Denmark, with a close relationship with the sea. The square, which is designed to accommodate different recreational activities, is formed by a composition of concrete blocks on top of a pool of water, as though the bay is flowing into town.

0994 West 8 created a park for Buona Vista, a suburb of Singapore. The site, defined by a dramatic topography and interesting sightlines, provides a place for leisure with tropical plants and trees. The highlight of the park is a monumental water feature formed by a stream that flows uphill.

0995 The existing walkway in a private residence in Key West, Florida, has been transformed into a series of stone slabs that seem to float on a small water garden. A waterfall fed by one-horsepower pump tumbles into the water garden.

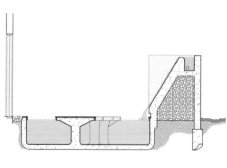

Section through water garden

0996

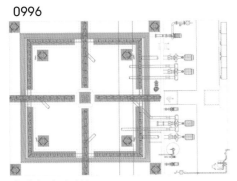

Detail plan of water inlet

▽

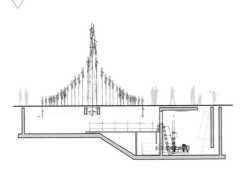

Section through water inlet

▷

0996 Jean Max Llorca designed a fountain based on the geometry of the Golden Section for la Place du Nombre d'Or in Montpellier, France. The fountain is composed of an interplay of squares and triangles formed by vertical jets of water.

0997 A plot that was previously occupied by a mansion has become a park with seats, balance bars and an interactive fountain that has been molded from recovered material.

0998 At the Diana, Princess of Wales Memorial Fountain, the water rushes turbulent in some parts but flows smoothly through the granite trough. This is achieved by the different textures of the blocks of Cornish granite that compose the ring.

0999 A concrete canal leads to a galvanized steel scupper and a concrete wall that serves as a dam. Rather than conflicting with the natural setting, this wall harmonizes with the vegetation thanks to stains caused by water dripping down its surface.

1000 The theme of reflection is explored at different levels: first through the surroundings reflected in the chrome balls, and second, through the reflection of these balls in the pond.

0001, 0060, 0061, 0062
1:1 landskab
www.1til1landskab.dk
© 1:1 landskab
0002, 0274, 0594, 0639, 0640, 0641,
0715, 0721, 0783, 0785
3:0 Landschaftsarchitektur
www.3zu0.com
© 3:0 Landschaftsarchitektur (0002, 0274,
0594, 0639, 0640, 0641, 0715)
© Paul Weihs (0721)
© Rupert Steiner (0783, 0785)
0003, 0065, 0066, 0456, 0457, 0644
100 Landschaftsarchitektur
www.100land.de
© 100 Landschaftsarchitektur
0004, 0007, 0008, 0068, 0070, 0073, 0181, 0384,
0385, 0460, 0595, 0596, 0645, 0720, 0951
Bruto Landscape Architecture
www.bruto.si
© Miran Kambič (0004, 0008, 0181, 0595)
© Matej Kučina (0007, 0068, 0070, 0384, 0385, 0645)
© Miran Kambič, Matej Kučina (0073, 0460, 0596, 0951)
0005, 0069, 0179, 0216, 0318, 0321
Batlle i Roig Arquitectes
www.batlleiroig.com
© Eva Serrats (0005)
© Wenzel Photographers (0069)
© Jorge Poo (0179, 0321)
© Jordi Surroca (0216, 0318)
0006, 0071, 0199, 0383
Beth Galí/BB + GG arquitectes
www.bethgali.com
© Beth Galí/BB + GG arquitectes (0006, 0071, 0383)
© Monika Gora (0199)
0007 (0004)
0008 (0004)
0009, 0010, 0093, 0285, 0322, 0464, 0539,
0598, 0653, 0835, 0836, 0840, 0952, 0953
Francis Landscapes Sal. Offshore
www.francislandscapes.com
© Francis Landscapes Sal. Offshore
0010 (0009)
0011, 0090, 0091, 0092, 0252, 0506
Habitat Landscape Architects
www.habitatdesign.co.za
© Habitat Landscape Architects
0012, 0323, 0538, 0541, 0544, 0545
Gora Art & Landscape
www.gora.se
© Monika Gora (0012, 0323, 0544)
© Fredrik Karlsson (0538)
© Björn Ullhagen (0541)
© Peo Olsson (0545)
0013, 0014, 0094
Häfner/Jiménez Büro für Landschaftsarchitektur
www.haefner-jimenez.de
© Häfner/Jiménez Büro für Landschaftsarchitektur
0014 (0013)
0015, 0016, 0182, 0324, 0838, 0839
Ioakim-Loizas Architects Engineers
www.ioloarchitects.com
© Ioakim-Loizas Architects Engineers
0016 (0015)
0017, 0046, 0096, 0102, 0173, 0395, 0396,
0397, 0465, 0711, 0712, 0713, 0714
Idealice
www.idealice.at
© Idealice
0018, 0050, 0099, 0101, 0255, 0282, 0325, 0326, 0328,
0331, 0375, 0398, 0654, 0656, 0729, 0842, 0959, 0961
Jos van de Lindeloof
www.josvandelindeloof.nl
© Jos van de Lindeloof

0019, 0329
KLA Kamphans Landscape Architecture
www.kamphans.com
© KLA Kamphans Landscape Architecture
0020, 0400
Ishtmus Urbanism Design | Landscape Architecture
www.isthmus.co.nz
© Ishtmus Urbanism Design | Landscape Architecture
0021, 0109, 0110, 0111, 0112, 0115,
0189, 0228, 0229, 0403, 0929
Landskap Design
www.landskapdesign.no
© Landskap Design (0021, 0403)
© Arne Sælen (0109, 0110, 0111, 0112,
0115, 0189, 0228, 0229, 0929)
0022, 0024, 0049, 0113, 0117, 0257, 0259, 0261, 0262,
0292, 0330, 0332, 0509, 0738, 0739, 0740, 0963
Mayer/Reed
www.mayerreed.com
© Mayer/Reed
0023, 0327
MADE associati | architettura e paesaggio
www.madeassociati.it
© MADE associati | architettura e paesaggio
0024 (0022)
0025, 0027, 0119, 0405
Newtown Landscape Architects
www.newla.co.za
© Newtown Landscape Architects
0026, 0043, 0156, 0207, 0230, 0270, 0495, 0805, 0826
McGregor Coxall
www.mcgregorcoxall.com
© McGregor Coxall (0026, 0230)
© Agnese Sanvito, Christian Brochert (0043, 0495)
© Simon Wood (0156, 0805)
© Brett Boardman (0207, 0270)
© Christian Borchert (0826)
0027 (0025)
0028, 0030, 0120, 0121, 0122, 0125, 0188, 0215,
0275, 0337, 0338, 0341, 0348, 0402, 0404, 0405,
0546, 0548, 0588, 0589, 0628, 0964, 0965
Okra Landschapsarchitecten
www.okra.nl

© Ben Ter Mull (0028, 0348, 0546, 0548,
0588, 0589, 0628, 0964, 0965)
© Okra Landschapsarchitecten (0030, 0120, 0121, 0122, 0125,
0188, 0215, 0275, 0337, 0338, 0341, 0402, 0404, 0405)
0029, 0051, 0116, 0273, 0362, 0438,
0439, 0661, 0804, 0818, 0822
Thomas Oslund/oslund.and.assoc.
www.oaala.com
© Michael Mingo, Tom Oslund (0029, 0439, 0661)
© George Heinrich, Tadd Kreun, Peter Vevang (0051)
© Thomas Oslund/oslund.and.assoc. (0116, 0804, 0822)
© Worldgymrank, oslund.and.assoc., Tadd
Kreun, Jerry Hom, Amy Krautbauer (0273)
© George Heinrich, Tadd Kreun (0362)
© Tom Oslund, George Heinrich, Jerry Hom (0438, 0818)
0030 (0028)
0031, 0743
Osa architettura e paesaggio
www.osaweb.it
© Osa architettura e paesaggio
0032, 0052, 0512, 0967
R&R Rencoret y Ruttimann Arquitectura y Paisaje
www.rencoretyruttimann.cl
© R&R Rencoret y Ruttimann Arquitectura y Paisaje
0033, 0183, 0339, 0476, 0551
Rankinfraser Landscape Architecture
www.rankinfraser.com
© Rankinfraser Landscape Architecture (0033, 0339, 0476)
© Dave Morris Photography (0183, 0551)
0034, 0126, 0305, 0336

RGA Arquitectes
www.rga.es
© RGA Arquitectes (0034, 0126, 0336)
© RGA Arquitectes, Lourdes Jansana (0305)
0035, 0133, 0412, 0432, 0478, 0549, 0660, 0742
Rios Clementi Hale Studios
www.rchstudios.com
© Rios Clementi Hale Studios (0035, 0133)
© Scott Shingley (0412)
© Tom Bonner (0432, 0549, 0742)
© Carlson & Co. (0478)
© John Ellis (0660)
0036, 0134, 0185, 0190, 0235, 0276, 0417, 0659
Schweingruber Zulauf Landschaftsarchitekten
www.schweingruberzulauf.ch
© Schweingruber Zulauf Landschaftsarchitekten
0037, 0056, 0057, 0139, 0233, 0236, 0662, 0663
Shades of Green Landscape Architecture
www.shadesofgreenla.com
© Shades of Green Landscape Architecture
0038, 0138, 0186, 0191, 0298, 0664, 0665, 0666, 0668
Simon Rackham Landscape Architects
www.simonrackham.com
© Simon Rackham Landscape Architects
0039, 0151, 0302, 0753, 0756, 0758, 0759, 0760, 0762
Verdier Landscape Design Studio Corporate House Building
www.estudiopaisajisticoverdier.com
© Verdier Landscape Design Studio Corporate House Building
0040
WOHA
http://wohadesigns.com
© Patrick Bingham-Hall
0041
Jensen Architects
http://jensen-architects.com
© Marion Brenner
0042, 0264
Atelier du Pont
www.atelierdupont.fr
© Luc Boegly
0043 (0026)
0044, 0132, 0411, 0475, 0477, 0481, 0552
Land by Sandra Aguilar
sandrajaguilar.blogspot.com
© Land by Sandra Aguilar
0045, 0079, 0223, 0251, 0283, 0390, 0392
Carve
www.carve.nl
© Carve
0046 (0017)
0047, 0114, 0471, 0474, 0734, 0736, 0737, 0962
Lodewijk Baljon
www.baljon.nl
© Rik Klein Gotink (0047, 0114)
© Lodewijk Baljon (0471, 0474, 0736, 0962)
© Daniel Nicolas (0734)
0048, 0100, 0103, 0807, 0903
Karres en Brands
www.karresenbrands.nl
© Karres en Brands (0048, 0100, 0103, 0807)
© Karres en Brands, Jeroen Musch (0903)
0049 (0022)
0050 (0018)
0051 (0029)
0052 (0032)
0053, 0147, 0346, 0420, 0586, 0587, 0626,
0707, 0716, 0757, 0928, 0932
Taylor Cullity Lethlean
www.tcl.net.au
© Taylor Cullity Lethlean (0053, 0147, 0420, 0626)
© Taylor Cullity Lethlean, John Gollings,
Peter Hyatt (0346, 0586)
© Taylor Cullity Lethlean, Michael
Nicholson, Brett Boardman (0587)

© Taylor Cullity, Lethlean, Peter Hyatt, Ben Wrigley, Diana Snape (0707, 0932)
© John Gollings (0741)
© Peter Hyatt (0757)
© Ben Wrigley, Carla Gottgens (0809)
0054, 0187, 0408, 0409, 0623, 0745, 0747, 0825, 0936
RMP Stephan Lenzen Landschaftsarchitekten
www.rmp-landschaftsarchitekten.de
© RMP Stephan Lenzen Landschaftsarchitekten

0055, 0300, 0421, 0422, 0425, 0484, 0555, 0971
Thomas Balsley Associates
www.tbany.com
© Thomas Balsley Associates
0056 (0037)
0057 (0037)
0058, 0834
Arteks
http://arteks.ad
© Emili Sardà (0058)
© Pedro Pegenaute (0834)
0059, 0524
R&Sie(n) Architects
www.new-territories.com
© R&Sie(n) Architects
0060 (0001)
0061 (0001)
0062 (0001)
0063, 0064, 0642, 0717
1moku co. Modern Garden Design
www.1moku.co.jp
© 1moku co. Modern Garden Design
0064 (0063)
0065 (0003)
0066 (0003)
0067, 0716
Vito Acconci/Acconci Studio
www.acconci.com
© Vito Acconci/Acconci Studio
0068 (0004)
0069 (0005)
0070 (0004)
0071 (0006)
0072, 0164, 0205, 0307, 0317, 0380, 0381, 0437, 0450, 0459, 582, 0808
ASPECT Studios
www.aspect.net.au
© ASPECT Studios (0072, 0317, 0380, 0381, 0450, 0459, 0582)
© Kyla Sheehan, Simon Wood, Terence Chin (0164)
© Simon Wood (0205, 0808)
© Florian Groehn (0307, 0437)
0073 (0004)
0074, 0080, 0210, 0247, 0248, 0249, 0253, 0360, 0387, 0440, 0442
Paolo Bürgi
www.burgi.ch
© Paolo Bürgi (0074, 0080, 0210, 0247, 0248, 0249, 0253, 0387)
© Paolo Bürgi, Giosanna Crivelli, Mei Wu (0360)
© Paolo Bürgi, Giosanna Crivelli, Dinah-Florentine Schmidt, Thomas Gut (0440)
© Giosanna Crivelli (0442)
0075, 0076, 0078, 0172, 0175, 0218, 0250, 0281, 0389, 0461, 0463, 0719
Cardinal Hardy
www.cardinal-hardy.ca
© Cardinal Hardy
0076 (0075)
0077, 0177, 0386, 0646, 0648, 0697, 0698
Burger Landschaftsarchitekten
www.burgerlandschaftsarchitekten.de
© Rakete (0077)
© Gerrit Engel (0177)

© Boris Storz (0386)
© Burger Landschaftsarchitekten (0646)
© Michael Heinrich (0648)
© Florian Holzherr, Burger Landschaftsarchitekten, Rakete (0697, 0698)
0078 (0075)
0079 (0045)
0080 (0074)
0081, 0084, 0220, 0221, 0289, 0315, 0391, 0534, 0597
C. F. Møller
www.cfmoller.com
© C. F. Møller
0082, 0085, 0087, 0178, 0226, 0284, 0319, 0320, 0393
Earthscape
www.earthscape.co.jp
© Earthscape
0083, 0466, 0505, 0724
Fabio Márquez
www.fabiomarquez.com.ar
© Fabio Márquez
0084 (0081)
0085 (0082)
0086, 0222, 0254, 0394, 0650, 0651
Gerhard Rennhofer/Landschaftsarchitektur
www.landschaftsarchitekt.at
© Landschaftsarchitektur
0087 (0082)
0088, 0089, 0399, 0462
East
www.east.uk.com
© East
0089 (0088)
0090 (0011)
0091 (0011)
0092 (0011)
0093 (0009)
0094 (0013)
0095, 0938
Hosper Landschapsarchitectuur en Stedebouw
http://hosper.nl
© Hosper Landschapsarchitectuur en Stedebouw (0095)
© Pieter Kers (0938)
0096 (0017)
0097, 0098, 0169, 0192, 0258, 0468, 0580, 0655, 0686, 0687, 0731, 0912
Janet Rosenberg + Associates
www.jrala.ca
© Janet Rosenberg + Associates (0097, 0098, 0192, 0655, 0731, 0912)
© Neil Fox, Jan Becker (0169, 0580)
© Neil Fox (0686, 0687)
0098 (0097)
0099 (0018)
0100 (0048)
0101 (0018)
0102 (0017)
0103 (0048)
0104, 0107, 0108, 0312, 0657, 0733, 0735, 0844
Landlab
www.landlab.nl
© Landlab
0105, 0106, 0180, 0290, 0291, 0469, 0470, 0472, 0473, 0629, 0706
LAND-I Archicolture
www.archicolture.com
© LAND-I Archicolture
0106 (0105)
0107 (0104)
0108 (0104)
0109 (0021)
0110 (0021)
0111 (0021)
0112 (0021)
0113 (0022)

0114 (0047)
0115 (0021)
0116 (0029)
0117 (0022)
0118, 0234, 0295, 0547
N-tree Contemporary Art & Landscape Garden
www.n-tree.jp
© N-tree Contemporary Art & Landscape Garden (0118, 0234, 0295)
© Michael Freeman (0547)
0119 (0025)
0120 (0028)
0121 (0028)
0122 (0028)
0123, 0184, 0333, 0335, 0407, 0410, 0413, 0827, 0931
Rehwaldt Landschaftsarchitekten
www.rehwaldt.net
© Rehwaldt Landschaftsarchitekten
0124, 0127, 0510, 0511, 0744
PEG office of landscape + architecture
www.peg-ola.com
© PEG office of landscape + architecture
0125 (0028)
0126 (0034)
0127 (0124)
0128, 0129, 0130, 0131, 0174, 0845
Richard Koek/Rijnboutt
www.rijnboutt.nl
© Richard Koek/Rijnboutt
0129 (0128)
0130 (0128)
0131 (0128)
0132 (0044)
0133 (0035)
0134 (0036)
0135, 0297, 0414, 0453
Sasaki
www.sasaki.com
© Sasaki
0136, 0137, 0140, 0141, 0415, 0451, 0452, 0556, 0608, 0667, 0748
Stephen Diamond Associates
www.sdacla.ie
© Stephen Diamond Associates
0137 (0136)
0138 (0038)
0139 (0037)
0140 (0136)
0141 (0136)
0142, 0144, 0296, 0334, 0537, 0609, 0670, 0746, 0749, 0750, 0751, 0846, 0968
SWA Group
www.swagroup.com
© SWA Group (0142, 0144, 0296, 0334, 0537, 0609, 0670, 0750, 0751, 0968)
© Tom Fox (0746, 0749, 0846)
0143, 0145, 0146, 0163, 0197, 0198, 0266, 0299, 0303, 0311, 0340, 0347, 0377, 0418, 0482, 0610, 0752, 0918, 0920, 0921, 0924, 0925, 0939, 0969, 0993
Birk Nielsen/Sweco Architects (0143, 0145, 0146, 0163, 0266, 0377, 0610, 0752, 0918, 0920, 0921, 0924, 0925, 0969, 0993)
Thorbjörn Andersson/Sweco Architects (0197, 0198, 0299, 0303, 0311, 0418, 0939)
www.sweco.dk
© Sweco Architects (0143, 0145, 0146, 0163, 0197, 0198, 0266, 0299, 0303, 0311, 0340, 0377, 0418, 0482, 0752)
© Ake E:son Lindman, Pege Hillinge, Pelle Wichman (0340, 0939)
© Thorbjörn Andersson, Jan Olof Andersson, Pege Hillinge, Scanfix (0347)
© Birk Nielsen (0610, 0918, 0920, 0921, 0924, 0925, 0969, 0993)
0144 (0142)
0145 (0143)

0146 (0143)
0147 (0053)
0148, 0149, 0150, 0193, 0423
Topotek
www.topotek1.de
© Topotek
0149 (0148)
0150 (0148)
0151 (0039)
0152, 0485
Plant Architect
www.branchplant.com
© Plant Architect
0153, 0196, 0304, 0424, 0528, 0685, 0914
Grupo de Diseño Urbano (GDU)
www.gdu.com.mx
© Dixi Carrillo (0153, 0196, 0304)
© Carlos Hahn, Francisco Gómez Sosa (0424)
© Grupo de Diseño Urbano (GDU) (0528)
© Francisco Gómez Sosa, Grupo de Diseño
Urbano (GDU) (0685, 0914)
0154, 0431
Mateo Arquitectura
www.mateo-arquitectura.com
© Mateo Arquitectura
0155, 0377
Arriola & Fiol Arquitectes
http://arquitectes.coac.net
© Arriola & Fiol Arquitectes
0156 (0026)
0157
Urbanus
www.urbanus.com.cn
© Yan Meng, Jiu Chen
0158, 0240
Kristine Jensens Landscapearchitect
www.kristinejensen.dk
© Kristine Jensens Landscapearchitect
0159, 0239, 0502, 0503, 0585, 0622, 0817, 0820,
0901, 0923, 0926, 0927, 0928, 0930, 0933,
Atelier Dreiseitl
www.dreiseitl.de
© Atelier Dreiseitl
0160, 0162, 0208, 0764, 0770, 0816
Andrea Cochran
www.acochran.com
© Marion Brenner (0160, 0162, 0208, 0816)
© Andrea Cochran (0764, 0770)
0161, 0436
B.A.E.R.
© Stephan Becsi
0162 (0160)
0163 (0143)
0164 (0072)
0165
Tillner & Willinger
www.tw-arch.at
© Monica Nikolic
0166, 0699, 0871, 0873, 0905
Lundberg Design
www.lundbergdesign.com
© Lundberg Design (0166, 0699, 0871)
© César Rubio (0873)
© J. D. Peterson, Troels Laerke (0905)
0167, 0170, 0238, 0242
Kendle Design Collaborative
www.kendledesign.com
© Rick Brazil
0168
Mauricio Rocha Taller de Arquitectura
http://tallerdearquitectura.com.mx
© Sandra Pereznieto
0169 (0097)
0170 (0167)

0171
OAB Office of Architecture Barcelona
www.ferrater.com
© ASCER
0172 (0075)
0173 (0017)
0174 (0128)
0175 (0075)
0176, 0219, 0388
Bureau B+B
www.bplusb.nl
© Bureau B+B
0177 (0077)
0178 (0082)
0179 (0005)
0180 (0105)
0181 (0004)
0182 (0015)
0183 (0033)
0184 (0123)
0185 (0036)
0186 (0038)
0187 (0054)
0188 (0028)
0189 (0021)
0190 (0036)
0191 (0038)
0192 (0097)
0193 (0148)
0194, 0265, 0342, 0672
Tegnestuen Schul Landskabsarkitekter
http://schul.dk
© Tegnestuen Schul Landskabsarkitekter
0195, 0638, 0799
Rush Wright Associates
www.rushwright.com
© Michael Wright, David Simmonds (0195, 0799)
© Derek Swalwell, Peter Bennetts (0638)
0196 (0153)
0197 (0143)
0198 (0143)
0199 (0006)
0200, 0256, 0491, 0532
Oxigen Landscape Architects + Urban Designers
www.oxigen.net.au
© Eyefood Photography (0200, 0532)
© N.A. (0256)
© Greg Healy (0491)
0201, 0578, 0617, 0634, 0684, 0810, 0911, 0913
SLA
www.sla.dk
© SLA (0201, 0578, 0684, 0810, 0911)
© SLA, Torben Petersen (0617)
© Jens Lindhe (0634)
0202, 0841, 0946, 0955, 0956, 0957, 0958, 0992, 0996
JML Consultants (0202, 0841, 0955,
0956, 0957, 0958, 0992, 0996)
www.jmlwaterfeaturedesign.com
Toyo Ito & Architects Associates,
JML Consultants (0946)
www.toyo-ito.co.jp
© Stéphane Llorca
0203, 0579, 0688, 0767, 0811, 0813, 0915, 0916
Delta Vorm Groep
www.deltavormgroep.nl
© Frank Colder, Picture 7 (0203)
© Frank Colder (0579, 0688, 0811, 0813, 0915, 0916)
© Delta Vorm Groep (0767)
0204
Estudio del Paisaje Teresa Moller & Asociados
http://teresamoller.cl
© Estudio del Paisaje Teresa Moller & Asociados
0205 (0072)
0206

Gualtiero Oberti
www.gualtierooberti.it
© Gualtiero Oberti
0207 (0026)
0208 (0160)
0209, 0441, 0542
James Carpenter
www.jcdainc.com
© Andreas Keller
0210 (0074)
0211
Payette Associates
www.payette.com
© Payette Associates
0212
Atelier Feichang Jianzhu
www.fcjz.com
© Fu, Xing
0213
Turnbull Griffin Haesloop
http://tgharchitects.com
© David Wakely
0214, 0244, 0443
Michele & Miquel Architectes & Paysagistes
michele_miquel@telefonica.net
© Michele & Miquel Architectes & Paysagistes
0215 (0028)
0216 (0005)
0217, 0280, 0313, 0314, 0382, 0593
Brandt Landskab
www.brandtlandskab.dk
© Brandt Landskab
0218 (0075)
0219 (0176)
0220 (0081)
0221 (0081)
0222 (0086)
0223 (0045)
0224, 0225, 0287, 0288, 0467
Johansson Landskab
www.johanssonlandskab.dk
© Johansson Landskab
0225 (0224)
0226 (0082)
0227, 0527, 0599, 0600, 0837, 0954, 0998
Gustafson Porter
www.gustafson-porter.com
© Gustafson Porter (0227, 0837)
© Gustafson Porter, Helene Binet, Jannes
Linders, Jeroen Helle (0527)
© James Newton, Speirs & Major (0599, 0600)
© Barron Gould (0954)
© Helene Binet (0998)
0228 (0021)
0229 (0021)
0230 (0026)
0231
María Teresa Cervantes Joló
maitane@terra.com.pe
© María Teresa Cervantes Joló
0232
Site Office Landscape Architecture
www.siteoffice.com.au
© Ben Wrigley
0233 (0037)
0234 (0118)
0235 (0036)
0236 (0037)
0237, 0294, 0416, 0419, 0554
Strootman Landschapsarchitecten
www.strootman.net
© Strootman Landschapsarchitecten
0238 (0167)
0239 (0159)

0240 (0158)
0241
Kuhn Truninger Landschaftsarchitekten
www.kuhn-la.ch
© Ralph Feiner
0242 (0167)
0243
Rockhill and Associates
www.rockhillandassociates.com
© Patrick Coulie Photography
0244 (0214)
0245
Matías González, Rodrigo Searle
www.tierraatacama.com
© Hotel Tierra Atacama
0246
RCR Aranda Pigem Vilalta Arquitectes
www.rcrarquitectes.es
© Eugeni Pons
0247 (0074)
0248 (0074)
0249 (0074)
0250 (0075)
0251 (0045)
0252 (0011)
0253 (0074)
0254 (0086)
0255 (0018)
0256 (0200)
0257 (0022)
0258 (0097)
0259 (0022)
0260
Foreign Office Architects (FOA)
http://azpa.com
www.farshidmoussavi.com
© Nácasa & Partners, Satoru Mishima
0261 (0022)
0262 (0022)
0263
Oü Ab Kosmos
www.kosmoses.ee
© Ott Kadarik
0264 (0042)
0265 (0194)
0266 (0143)
0267, 0269, 0301, 0428, 0514, 0515, 0530,
0584, 0591, 0624, 0632, 0673, 0674, 0703
Turenscape
www.turenscape.com
© Turenscape (0267, 0269, 0301, 0428,
0514, 0515, 0673, 0674)
© Kongjian Yu, Cao Yang (0530, 0584, 0591, 0624, 0632)
© Kongjian Yu (0703)
0268, 0984
Josef Pleskot/AP Atelier
www.arch.cz/pleskot
© Jan Malý
0269 (0267)
0270 (0026)
0271, 0344, 0365, 0366, 0367, 0368
Feichtinger Architectes
www.feichtingerarchitectes.com
© Feichtinger Architectes (0271, 0365, 0366, 0368)
© David Boureau (0344)
0272, 0345
Jensen & Skodvin Arkitektkontor
www.jsa.no
© Jensen & Skodvin Arkitektkontor
0273 (0029)
0274 (0002)
0275 (0028)
0276 (0036)
0277, 0433

Tejo Remy & René Veenhuizen
www.remyveenhuizen.nl
© Herbert Wiggerman
0278, 0934, 0937, 0948, 0950
Bjørbekk & Lindheim
www.blark.no
© Bjørbekk & Lindheim (0278, 0934, 0937, 0950)
© Marte G. Johnsen (0948)
0279
C+S architects Carlo Cappai and Maria Alessandra Segantini
www.cipiuesse.it
© C+S architects Carlo Cappai and
Maria Alessandra Segantini
0280 (0217)
0281 (0075)
0282 (0018)
0283 (0045)
0284 (0082)
0285 (0009)
0286, 0725, 0726, 0728, 0732
Ilias Lolidis
www.studioland.gr
© Ilias Lolidis
0287 (0224)
0288 (0224)
0289 (0081)
0290 (0105)
0291 (0105)
0292 (0022)
0293, 0605, 0606, 0607, 0658, 0843, 0966
Scape Design Associates
www.scapeda.co.uk
© Scape Design Associates
0294 (0237)
0295 (0118)
0296 (0142)
0297 (0135)
0298 (0038)
0299 (0143)
0300 (0055)
0301 (0267)
0302 (0039)
0303 (0143)
0304 (0153)
0305 (0034)
0306
Guallart Architects
http://guallart.com
© Núria Díaz
0307 (0072)
0308
PLOT=BIG+JDS
www.big.dk
© Paolo Rosselli, Julien de Smed, Esben Bruun
0309, 0577, 0947
EDAW
www.aecom.com
© EDAW, Hai River Administration Bureau (0309)
© David Lloyd, Dixi Carrillo, Frank Chow/EDAW (0577)
© Dixi Carrillo/EDAW; Peter Matthews (0947)
0310, 0847
Verzone Woods Architectes
http://vwa.ch
© Craig Verzone/Verzone Woods Architectes, Nozar
0311 (0143)
0312 (0104)
0313 (0217)
0314 (0217)
0315 (0081)
0316, 0455
1/1 Architecture
www.onetooneistanbul.com
© 1/1 Architecture
0317 (0072)

0318 (0005)
0319 (0082)
0320 (0082)
0321 (0005)
0322 (0009)
0323 (0012)
0324 (0015)
0325 (0018)
0326 (0018)
0327 (0023)
0328 (0018)
0329 (0019)
0330 (0022)
0331 (0018)
0332 (0022)
0333 (0123)
0334 (0142)
0335 (0123)
0336 (0034)
0337 (0028)
0338 (0028)
0339 (0033)
0340 (0143)
0341 (0028)
0342 (0194)
0343
Xavier Font Solà/Alfa Polaris
http://bierot.net
© Xavier Font Solà
0344 (0271)
0345 (0272)
0346 (0053)
0347 (0143)
0348 (0028)
0349, 0500, 0533, 0611, 0755, 0970
Terragram
http://terragram.com.au
© Vladimir Sitta, Minitheater Productions (0349, 0500)
© Terragram (0611, 0755)
0350, 0351, 0709, 0823, 0994
West 8
www.west8.nl
© West 8 (0350, 0351, 0823, 0994)
© Jeroen Musch (0709)
0351 (0350)
0352
Germán del Sol
www.germandelsol.cl
© Guy Wenborne
0353
Juan Antonio Sánchez/Adhoc MSL
www.adhocmsl.com
© David Frutos
0354
Carl-Viggo Hølmebakk
www.holmebakk.no
© Carl-Viggo Hølmebakk, Rickard Riesenfeld
0355
Felipe Peña Pereda, Francisco Novoa Rodríguez
+34 981 221 974
© Juan Rodríguez
0356
Todd Saunders, Tommie Wilhelmsen
www.saunders-wilhelmsen.no
© Todd Saunders
0357, 0435, 0690
3LHD
www.3lhd.com
© Aljoša Brajdić (0357)
© Mario Jelavić, Domagoj Blažević (0435, 0690)
0358
Durbach Block Architects
http://durbachblockjaggers.com
© Kraig Carlstrom

Glasser und Dagenbach
www.glada-berlin.de
© Udo Dagenbach
0494
David A. García
http://davidgarciastudio.blogspot.com
© David A. García, Max Gerthel
0495 (0026)
0496
nArchitects
http://narchitects.com
© nArchitects
0497
Mauricio Cárdenas, Roberto Banfi,
Giacomo Schirru/Studio Cárdenas
www.studiocardenas.it
© Studio Cárdenas
0498
Casagrande Laboratory Taiwan
http://marcocasagrande.fi
© Hsieh Ying-Chun, Marco Casagrande, Roan Ching-Yueh
0499 (0429)
0500 (0349)
0501, 0619
Landworks Studio
www.landworks-studio.com
© Landworks Studio
0502 (0159)
0503 (0159)
0504, 0819, 0943, 0944
Michael Singer
www.michaelsinger.com
© Michael Singer (0504)
© K. D. Bus (0819)
© David Stansbury (0943, 0944)
0505 (0083)
0506 (0011)
0507, 0536, 0727
H+N+S Landschapsarchitecten
www.hnsland.nl
© H+N+S Landschapsarchitecten
0508, 0730
Irene Burkhardt Landschaftsarchitekten
http://www.irene-burkhardt.de
© Irene Burkhardt
0509 (0022)
0510 (0124)
0511 (0124)
0512 (0032)
0513, 0535, 0669
Spackman, Mossop + Michaels
www.mossopmichaels.com
© Spackman, Mossop + Michaels
0514 (0267)
0515 (0267)
0516, 0517, 0518, 0519
Gardena
www.gardena.com
© Gardena
0517 (0516)
0518 (0516)
0519 (0516)
0520, 0523, 0562, 0566, 0796, 0983
Stoss Landscape Urbanism
www.stoss.net
© Stoss Landscape Urbanism (0520,
0523, 0562, 0566, 0796)
© Jeff Mirkes (0983)
0521
Graf
www.grafiberica.com
© Graf
0522
Renzo Piano Building Workshop

www.rpbw.com
© Tim Griffith, Tom Fox
0523 (0520)
0524 (0059)
0525
David Baker + Partners Architects
www.dbarchitect.com
© David Baker + Partners Architects
0526, 0693, 0812, 0814, 0917, 0919
GTL Gnüchtel Triebswetter Landschaftsarchitekten
www.gtl-kassel.de
© Stephan Hadke, Raffaella Sirtoli
Schnell, Tobias Graneztky (0526)
© Tim Nolan, Michael Triebwetter (0693, 0917)
© Joerg Albin, GTL Gnüchtel Triebwetter
Landschaftsarchitekten (0812)
© Christoph Moeller, Galabau Emsland (0814, 0919)
0527 (0227)
0528 (0153)
0529, 0627
CMG Landscape Architecture
www.cmgsite.com
© CMG Landscape Architecture
0530 (0267)
0531, 0540
Mikyoung Kim
www.mikyoungkim.com
© Taeoh Kim
0532 (0200)
0533 (0350)
0534 (0081)
0535 (0513)
0536 (0507)
0537 (0142)
0538, (0012)
0539 (009)
0540 (0531)
0541 (0012)
0542 (0209)
0543, 0583
2b Architectes
www.2barchitectes.ch
© 2b Architectes
0544 (0012)
0545 (0012)
0546 (0028)
0547 (0118)
0548 (0028)
0549 (0035)
0550, 0553, 0564, 0565, 0567, 0601,
0602, 0603, 0604, 0612, 0616
Roger Narboni/Concepto
www.lightingacademy.org
© Xavier Boymond (0550)
© Concepto (0553, 0602, 0603, 0604)
© Agence Jacqueline Osty,
Roger Narboni (0564, 0565, 0567, 0612, 0616)
© Concepto, Zhongtai Lighting Group (0601)
0551 (0033)
0552 (0044)
0553 (0550)
0554 (0237)
0555 (0055)
0556 (0136)
0557
Marset
www.marset.com
© Marset
0558, 0563
Santa & Cole
www.santacole.com
© Santa & Cole
0559
Galeria Joan Gaspar

www.galeriajoangaspar.com
© Galeria Joan Gaspar
0560
Gandía Blasco
www.gandiablasco.com
© Gandía Blasco
0561
Rob Slewe
http://www.ylighting.com
© Ylighting
0562 (0520)
0563 (0558)
0564 (0550)
0565 (0550)
0566 (0520)
0567 (0550)
0568, 0569
Akira Kuryu + Partner, Lighting Planners Associates
http://kuryu.com
© Toshio Kaneko
0569 (0568)
0570, 0571
Saratoga Associates, Piet Oudolf
www.saratogaassociates.com
© Seth Ely, Carrie Snyder, Amy Barkow, Saratoga Associates
0571 (0570)
0572
Lighting Planners Associates
www.lighting.co.jp
© Toshio Kaneko
0573, 0574
United Visual Artists with Onepointsix
www.uva.co.uk
© United Visual Artists
0574 (0573)
0575
Alsop Architects
www.alsoparchitects.com
© Jeremy San
0576
Cecil Balmond, António Adão da Fonseca/Arup (0576)
www.arup.com
© Leonardo Finotti
0577 (0309)
0578 (0201)
0579 (0203)
0580 (0097)
0581, 0592
AllesWirdGut Architektur
www.alleswirdgut.cc
© Hertha Hurnaus
0582 (0072)
0583 (0543)
0584 (0267)
0585 (0159)
0586 (0053)
0587 (0053)
0588 (0028)
0589 (0028)
0590, 0635, 0636, 0637, 0824, 0828, 0829,
0830, 0831, 0832, 0833, 0942, 0945
TROP Terrains + Openspace
www.tropstudio.com
© Charkhrit Chartarsa (0590, 0635, 0636, 0637,
0829, 0830, 0831, 0832, 0833, 0945)
© Wison Tungthunya (0824)
© TROP Terrains + Openspace (0828, 0942)
0591 (0267)
0592 (0581)
0593 (0217)
0594 (0581)
0595 (0004)
0596 (0004)
0597 (0081)